Dear readers,

Every memory recorded in the various YOURS books of nostalgia is precious. After all, the moments you describe and the characters you revive would have been lost, had you not put pen to paper.

But there's something doubly poignant about the readers' recollections in this particular YOURS collection because so many of your tales are about the Second World War, when our very future was at stake.

Future generations will be delighted to read first-hand accounts recording tiny episodes in what was a global adventure, and to feel the 'human' aspects of service life shining out of hardship, uncertainty and fear.

People say that with a sense of humour you can get through anything. So many of our readers are living testimony to that claim - there was always time for a lark and a laugh whether you were a Land Army lass, a front-line soldier or getting knocked into shape on National Service.

We do hope you enjoy every word of this collection. Many thanks to all those readers who contributed and to the many readers whose memories had to be left out.

Neil

eil Patrick, Editor-in-Chief,
YOURS magazine

THE NEW RECRUITS

A NEW LIFE

ON MARCH 19, 1940, I got my call-up papers. I wasn't quite sure where I was going, as the railway warrant said: "Ayer... Air" and finally, no doubt after checking, "Ayr". So it was off to Scotland and the Infantry Training Centre at Ayr racecourse.

I remember the blacked-out railway station at King's Cross and saying goodbye to my mother, and then the start of the long journey north. There were 10 of us in the carriage, and in the dim light you could see we all had more than one thing in common, misty eyes and lumps in our throats.

To make things more cheerful, I put my suitcase (bought in Petticoat Lane for half-a-crown) on my knees, and suggested a game of nap to while the hours away. On arrival at Ayr station, I had won a few bob, and nine lasting friends.

We piled out of the train, baggy-eyed and hungry, to be met by a piper and two corporals who hollered at us in some foreign language.

Civilian shoes are murder for marching, especially with cheap cardboard soles, and by the time we had reached the racecourse, we had all 'had it'.

The smell of hot food had us sniffing the air, and we marched into a large building to booes and cries of 'You'll be sorry' from the soldiers already sitting down to the mid-day meal. I remember that first meal very well, and sometimes when having mince at home, I'm away back at Ayr.

Next morning, the sound of reveille through the loud-speakers blasted us up and out to the wash-basins, shivering and

stupefied. The shock of a cold water wash and shave jerked all of us back to reality.

We dressed in our new, stiff, baggy, naptha-smelling battledress, and paraded for breakfast. This consisted of one slice of bread, one small cube of margarine, one rasher, one concrete fried egg, and tomatoes, with plenty of hot tea.

Drinking tea in our shiny new mess-tins was quite hazardous and many a lad in trying to find his mouth, slopped it all down his tunic.

Another parade was for uniform alterations, then came the queue for the dreaded barber.

This gentleman was a civilian sadist, who politely enquired: "How would you like it?" and then proceeded with blunt electric clippers to painfully hack off about 90 per cent of one's hair. We speculated that he had fled from Australia after a lifetime of inept sheep shearing.

After dinner, the next parade was for jabs. We lined up outside the MO's office in a long, winding file stretching around the parade ground.

As the door opened to admit the next man, the biggest fellows slithered to the floor in a dead faint, only to be picked up and pushed forward by smaller comrades.

When my turn came, I entered gingerly, dropped my trousers, took off my underpants, and rolled up my sleeves. In one concerted movement, four medics got me - one in each buttock, and one in each arm.

We were surprised to find we were excused duties for 24 hours, and we soon found out why.

Gradually our arms and bottoms grew stiff with pain, and we were unable to move our arms or even sit down. I lay face downwards on my bed of straw, and waited hopefully for the Grim Reaper. But next morning, I felt a lot better. I was able to move and sit down.

It was a hard slog, and there were night exercises once a week.

I learned to use the liquid compass, but couldn't understand why, over the next six years, I never once handled one again.

Matt was my stable companion. After hearing the drill corporal boasting that it had taken him only six years to get his stripes, we were determined to bust his record. We swotted up like mad, and spent every spare moment checking and re-checking everything we had been taught.

After two weeks of bashing away, we were allowed out for a few hours in Ayr. Waiting for permission to leave the camp, we noticed that all the permanent staff wore kilts, and had to stand, legs astride, over a mirror set in the floor, before they could leave.

This oddity became clear in the toilet of a local pub when I stood next to a camp sergeant. It became obvious that nothing was worn underneath.

Round about the third week, the RSM told us that a few vacancies existed within the camp concert party. I joined The Racecourse Racketeers and spent many happy and exhausting weeks touring Kilmarnock, Ayr, and the local villages. The fact that there were female soldiers in the group added a little spice to an otherwise colourless life.

One day I had an experience that gave me a terrific thrill. We were drilling, and it suddenly dawned on us while the company was doing the drill movements 'Quick march. About turn. Halt', that we sounded as one man!

We looked at each other and realised that we had finally got it! From that moment on we started to thoroughly enjoy our drill. The drill corporal beamed, congratulated us, and told us we were the finest bunch of recruits he had ever trained - liar. We fell asleep happy that night.

At the end of our training, we were paraded for inspection. Some of us were asked questions, and answered correctly. One Welsh lad, asked: "What steps would you take if a German platoon suddenly appeared?" replied: "Bloody long ones, sir".

Then came the marching-out parade before the depot commanding officer. A very aged, be-medalled gentleman gave us a speech, probably written in the 1914-1918 war, which was intended to increase our patriotic ardour and put paid to the 'dreaded Boche'.

My section was approached, and informed that we were being drafted into a Battalion of the Seaforth Highlanders. Any man absenting himself between now and the draft movement would be treated as a deserter.

I was surprised to be approached by the company commander and told that I was going to be held at Ayr. I had no idea why.

The following day, Italy declared war and attacked an already-beaten France. There were riots in Ayr, and many shops with Italian-sounding names had their windows smashed.

In the depot, recruits with Italian parents were pulled out for screening. This left gaps in the drafts to be filled, and I was put back in the original draft going to the Seaforths.

This turned out to be the start of three very happy years with the 7th Battalion Seaforth Highlanders.

J A JOHNSON

NO KIDDING!

DURING the war, we had the best warning system anyone could wish for - Wilhelmina, a nanny-goat who got recruited to our troop somewhere in Belgium.

Whenever you heard her start to bleat, you could guarantee that shells would be landing within minutes. We never heard a thing until they exploded.

Wilhelmina found a billy-goat in Holland, got herself pregnant, and had triplets in the back of a British truck in Germany.

One of our lads wrote to a daily newspaper with the question: "Belgian mother, Dutch father, triplets born in a British truck in Germany - what nationality are they?" The answer came back: "Displaced persons - no kidding!"

FRED NICHOLLS

Below: Wilhelmina the nanny-goat with her comrades in C Troop, 128 Battery, 86th Anti-Tank Regiment

BASHFULNESS IN THE BILLET

THE first day of my National Service - September 27, 1948 - at RAF Padgate was a day I shall never forget. New recruits were marched around the place for medicals, inoculations, lectures, billet allocation, and kitting out. Everything was done in alphabetical order, so with a name like Adams I was always called first for everything.

When we were finally allowed to our billet after a very busy day, the sergeant's final words to us were: "Get some sleep - you've had a fairly quiet day. Tomorrow you start work!"

We sat around discussing the day's events, wondering what was going to happen next morning, and waiting for someone to make a move to get into bed. No-one seemed to want to get undressed. It was the first time away from home for many of us and we found it embarrassing to get stripped off in front of so many onlookers.

As 'lights out' approached, you could hear a mad scramble as shirts, socks and trousers were quickly taken off and thrown anywhere. Then there was a strange silence, as if everyone was relieved that the lights had gone out and we were able to get to bed.

We were all apprehensive about what would be in store for us over the next two years - but it turned out to be an experience I would not have missed.

KEN ADAMS

Below: Ken Adams is on the left of this group, photographed outside the camp cinema at RAF Manston in 1950

BREAKING AWAY

THE Second World War gave me a freedom not even contemplated by an only daughter who never questioned the authority of her parents.

I had boyfriends as well as girlfriends but they were just friends - cousins or members of our Bible class. Without having to be told, I instinctively knew that any romantic attachment would not be allowed. Even my parents' choice of a career for me in the Civil Service took into consideration the opportunity of a pension if I stayed unmarried.

One example of the attitude with which I had been brought up came in September, 1939, when my father and I were walking along London's Great West Road.

A convoy of trucks filled with young soldiers passed by. The lads whistled and waved and instinctively I turned my head away. I was surprised when my father scolded me, saying: "Don't you ever do that again - don't you realise you might be the last girl they ever set eyes on?" He had twice been wounded in the First World War and lost many of his friends. I was made to stop and think. I was just 17.

Shortly afterwards I was drafted to the Royal Enfield arsenal. I would have had to take lodgings but my parents successfully petitioned for me to get a different posting so I needn't leave home - their idea, not mine. I was sent to the Home Office in Whitehall, but when my department was evacuated to Bournemouth, my parents did not intervene. The war was loosening their hold over me.

Here I met soldiers and airmen and had the occasional date. As a complete innocent, my innate sense of what was 'nice' and what was 'not nice' kept me from unwanted physical encounters. At the age of 19, back in London, I learned the facts of life from a case file on rape.

I wore trousers for the first time while doing voluntary work out of office hours as a dispatch rider for the War Office. Eventually, in 1942, my request for release to join the WAAF was granted.

As a Clerk Special Duties many new experiences lay ahead of me. I was still very reserved and at first found the lack of privacy difficult to cope with.

Four other girls and I arrived after 24 hours of travelling at our first posting to find we were billeted in what had been a boys' prep school. We asked the orderly room sergeant if we could have a bath and were told we would find plenty of baths on the same floor as our dormitory.

We found one large room with about a dozen baths of varying shapes and sizes arranged round three sides, with the tap ends towards the centre. We looked at one another in dismay before common sense overcame our reticence.

We each chose a bath and because there were no pegs, made neat piles of our clothing and towels at the end of each bath. Ablutions over, on the count of three we all stood up together and pulled out the plugs. Out gushed the water onto the floor - carrying away with it our clothes and towels towards a drainage hole in the centre of the room which we had not previously noticed. This incident forged a firm friendship between the five of us.

I flew as a passenger for the first time in 1944, hedge-hopping in a Dakota over French fields to join Eisenhower's HQ (SHAEF) in Versailles.

We were within reach of Paris. Although we were issued with trousers, we were banned from wearing them on duty or in the streets to avoid offence to the French population.

The little French plumber who dealt with problems in the barracks we occupied caused us more amusement than embarrassment whenever he came through our shower room on way to the boiler room. The showers had no curtains or screens and he would raise his hat to us as he passed, saying: "Bonjour, mademoiselles. Aaah! Les jeunes mademoiselles!" As we only had cold water for our showers, we often wondered why he was there.

Meeting Americans, French and other nationalities widened my insight into other ways of life. In Germany in 1945, I met an airman with whom I celebrated 50 golden years of marriage.

This love match did not meet with my parents' approval, but while I never lost my filial affection for them and always remembered their many good lessons, my release from their influence and control was at last achieved. Just six vital years - but they changed my life.

JACQUELINE RAWLINGS

NAMES, NOT NUMBERS

AT RASPE (The Rhine Army School of Preliminary Education) at Bielefeld, the Army tried to help illiterate or semi-illiterate young conscripts.

During my national service from 1947-1949, I was a sergeant in the education corps stationed there and we tried to give the new recruits a basic grounding in English and maths.

There were many Poles attached to the British Army who had fought against the Germans but who did not dare return home for fear of persecution by the Communists.

One morning after returning from leave, I was put on roll-call duty. When I got to the last twenty names, I was faced with a list of names full of 'V's, 'W's, 'Y's and 'Z's.

A group of Poles had been sent to the school to improve their English. As I hadn't the faintest idea how to pronounce their names and hoping they knew enough English to understand, I said I would read out the last three figures of their army numbers. This worked, and I dismissed them to their classes.

Between that day and my next roll-call duty, I spent quite a lot of time with the German clerk on the office staff, practising until I had learned to pronounce all the Polish names correctly.

When it came round, I read out all the English names, then proceeded to rattle off the Polish ones.

It was worth all that time and trouble to see some of the biggest grins I have ever seen - all because someone had taken the time and trouble to learn those Polish soldiers' names instead of treating them as numbers.

STAN FLYNN

Land Army girls on church parade. This picture was kindly sent in by Iris Ryan.

THE DOGS OF WAR

'DESERT Rats' was, of course, what they called the men of the Eighth Army, but there were also 'Desert Dogs' - real dogs.

Although they were unofficial companions, they were trusty ones, especially when we were on guard duty or driving trucks across the western deserts of North Africa.

One very special dog was Jess, a small terrier. She joined our Royal Army Service Corps (550 RASC) Company in Sarafand, Palestine, in February, 1940, and crossed the Suez Canal to join the famous Desert Rats 7th Armoured Division.

In July 1941, she was besieged in Tobruk and eventually rescued by the Australians. She sailed to safety in HMS

Vendetta to Alexandria, re-equipping at El Tanag, a large staging area near the Suez Canal.

In January, 1942, Jess found time to have puppies at an outpost by Agedabia near Tripolitania.

Being internationally-minded, she withdrew from the notorious battle of Bir Hacheim in May, 1942, with the help of the Free French Foreign Legion, escaping down to the Quattara Depression to await further instructions.

On the arrival of General Montgomery, Jess and our company were transferred from the 7th to the 10th Armoured Division, and just prior to the last of the desert campaigns - the Battle of Alamein - they joined the 1st Armoured Division, going forward to Tobruk, Benghazi, Agedabia, Tripoli, parading for the Royal General Lyon (King George VI), and doing Monty's left-hook battle with the New Zealanders to the hot springs of El Hamma in Tunisia.

Continuing on to Hamman Lif by the Palace of the Bey of Tunis, Jess produced more pups. Then we were off to Tunis, and then over the border to Algeria.

It was while we wintered at Bene Mered, edged by the snow-capped Atlas mountains, that Jess picked up some poison intended for rats - real rats - and died. She was a true companion and was missed by all.

If any dog qualified for the Africa Star medal and Eighth Army clasp, it was Jess - she fully earned and deserved one.

One of Jess's sons was Busty, born at Agedabia, in January 1942.

A fat, ugly, but lovable short-legged dog - a Heinz 57 varieties - he was predominately dachshund.

Busty was a very independent dog and would often disappear for days, or even weeks, before suddenly reappearing, completely out of the blue.

It was suggested that he was a German Afrika Korps spy dog - an idea which sparked lots of fun! One day he disappeared, never to be seen again - presumably a victim of the minefields.

After the invasion of Italy, Patch, a black and white mongrel dog, adopted me on the slopes of San Gennaro, Vesuvius, early in 1946, the year of the terrifying volcanic eruption.

He travelled with us to Naples, Cassino, Rome, Siena, Florence and up to the stalemate of the Germans' Gothic Line.

My repatriation to the UK came through after nearly five years abroad and I was left with the dilemma as to what to do with Patch. Reluctantly, I requested the loan of our officer's revolver, but our cook volunteered to look after him - which he did until Patch was run over and killed by a tank near Venice.

All these dogs and many more helped to boost morale and create companionship and interest among the troops during those long, tedious and often dangerous days of war.

HARRY STEER

SURVIVING MR SADE

AFTER the initial shock, I quite enjoyed my basic training on National Service. I had never smoked nor drank, and had entered the army straight from grammar school. I was as lean as a yard of pump-water and fit as a fiddle - a complete contrast to most of the intake, who coughed and gasped their way through every exercise.

An early lesson was that NCOs used an obscenity with every sentence, and that officers were akin to the Almighty. "If it moves, salute it! If it doesn't, whitewash it" was the credo for the first few weeks.

In the bitter, freezing weather, the top layer of coal in our bunker was whitewashed.

Every day we had to draw the regulation two buckets of coal for the billet and every night we had to sneak them back into the coalyard - woe betide anyone who disturbed the whitewash, or sullied the shining black belly of the stove by letting it get hot! "Cold? Then it's your own fault. You draw two buckets of coal each day and that's enough to keep anyone warm."

The majority of the NCOs were old sweats who had come through the war. Most of them made no bones about hating National Servicemen.

Blackdown, Farnborough and the depot battalion at Dover followed one another in quick succession. It was at Dover that I met an officer whom I shall call Mr Sade.

He would delight in walking behind the parade and bashing the large pack against the back of a soldier's head. Inevitably stumbling forward, the unfortunate would be put on a charge for moving on parade. Sade would mercilessly grind his heels on lovingly-polished toe-caps, push his evil face within an inch of the victim, and bellow: "You're a disgrace! Look at your boots!"

I fell foul of him when I had a throat infection and lost my voice. He walked round and round me, 'accidentally' knocking against me and screaming at the top of his voice: "You're bloody useless! Didn't you hear me? Lost your voice? Then bloody well look for it. Go on! Look for it! Double round the parade ground!"

When several circuits of the ground failed to put me out of breath, he went purple in the face and put me on a charge of leaving the parade without permission. I had a lump on the back of my head where my pack had been slammed into it.

Even at this late stage I still live in hope that one day I shall meet Mr Sade again, preferably walking across the road in front of my car. He was the Flashman of Dover, hated by everyone, and it was little wonder that he was never seen on his own.

PETER GASTON

12

DESPERATE REMEDY

I WENT to Manton hostel outside Oakham, Rutland, as a member of the Women's Land Army. It was a lovely old house with 20 girls and a warden, and I spent a very happy year there, though it was hard work.

My bunk mate Olive and I got creepy-crawlies in our hair, and although we scratched, washed and combed ourselves, there was no relief.

As a last resort, I got some sheep dip from a local farmer. He told me to dilute it, but I said to Olive: "This is either kill or cure" - and poured some over my head neat.

I think I jumped higher than any athlete, and shot into the garden to cool off. It certainly killed the crawlies and nearly finished me off as well!

The other girls thought it was hilarious and I never lived the episode down.

EILEEN WARRINER

Eileen Warriner has hair-raising memories of a sheep dip hair rinse

MEMORY OF CHANGI POWS

DURING the war I served in the RAF with 7017 Servicing Echelon/155 Spitfire Squadron in Burma, and afterwards in Singapore and Sumatra. Our squadron was the last on active service in the Far East and was not disbanded until July, 1946.

We arrived in Singapore immediately after the signing of the peace treaty by Lord Mountbatten, and one of our first duties was to help in the evacuation of POWs from Changi prison.

My memory of this episode is that when helping an Australian POW to the evacuation aircraft, he tripped and cut his knee. I bound it up with my handkerchief.

Being a bit of a sentimentalist, I have always liked to think that somewhere in Australia there was someone with a bloodstained handkerchief as a memento of his release from the Japanese prison at Changi.

ALBERT BENNETT

Above: Albert Bennett in uniform
Right: Albert in Sumatra, 1945

14

SUFFERING SPROGS

IT was January 1942, bitterly cold and I was a sprog, a new recruit to the RAF.

We stood in full battle order with heavy packs, Lee Enfield rifles (no ammunition), and bayonets; wearing our greatcoats and those forage caps which we soon learned to put on our shining Brylcreemed hair at an angle that seemed to defy the laws of gravity.

The snow swirled around and we looked like decorations on a Christmas cake. Our feet were sore in huge new

boots, but after about two hours the welcome order came to march off.

Guiding us down one of the quieter back streets, our drill corporal gave a bark which brought us all to a halt and then gave that blessed benediction: "Fall out, you worshippers at the shrine of nicotine".

Fags appeared as if by magic and soon the air was like a solid block of tobacco smoke. One of the bolder lads asked the corporal what the march and standing to attention had been in aid of. This brought the flicker of a smile to the corporal's face. "That, laddie, is to get you used to being buggered about - you'll get lots of it in future". How right he was!

Looking back, I have to admire the civilians who lived in Blackpool during the war years. A mass of light blue descended on the town like a science fiction plague. Of course, some of the citizens must have made a few bob in shops and pubs - we were very fit and active, and always hungry.

One of the best examples of enterprise was a bloke in a shop with a powered emery wheel who, for a small fee, would take your cap badge and buttons and buff off their 'new' look. Afterwards we all thought we looked like real veterans.

We were taught to use the bayonet in combat much as our fathers had used it in Flanders over 20 years before. I don't know if we were a particularly stupid-looking squad but our drill sergeant took one look at us and bawled: "Think I'm trusting you lot with naked bayonets? Not bloody likely!" So we did our drill with bayonets still in their scabbards.

Off duty we sat in pubs (we didn't drink a lot - the pay wouldn't run to it), picked up girls and took them dancing. But the most popular recreation, by far, was the cinema.

Imagine a cinema packed mainly with airmen, all entranced by that great film Sun Valley Serenade. When it came to Chattanooga Choo Choo, our exuberance really let rip - we sang, clapped and stamped our feet.

Although there was a concentration on PT and 'square bashing' our real training was to follow a trade. Mine was as a wireless operator, so with dozens of other hopefuls I sat on hard seats in the Winter Gardens being instructed in the mysteries of Morse Code.

If you could reach the required proficiency in Morse, and meet the rigorous medical standards, you might be accepted for air crew. Then you would be given the rank of sergeant and be classified as WOP/AG (Wireless Operator, Air Gunner).

So as we studied we often sang a little jingle to the tune of It's Foolish But It's Fun. It went something like this: 'I want to be a WOP/AG/ And fly all over Germany'. Many did not reach the standard in Morse, which meant 're-mustering' or applying to take up another trade. I failed my Morse exam and moved to southern England to train in another capacity.

DENNIS SHEWARD

THE HAND OF FATE

IN the 1930s, my sister Jessie was given a gold signet ring with the initial 'J' on it, a birthday present from Aunt Alice.

In 1938, when I was 18, Jessie gave the ring to me before I went to Hastings to visit my fiancee Lily, who later became my wife.

In 1940, I was called up in the Rifle Brigade. We were shipped out to North Africa and were involved in the North African campaign. Much to my dismay, while I was in Algiers I lost the gold signet ring.

We were moved on to Italy - by this time I was in the York and Lancs Regiment - and hostilities in Europe were coming to an end.

We were on parade when I noticed a Guardsman in front of me wearing a gold ring on his little finger. I said to him: "Excuse me, but has that ring you are wearing got the initial 'J' on it?" Without hesitation, he said yes, he had found it in the ablutions block at Bois-de-Boulogne in Algiers.

He immediately gave me the ring, and we warmly shook hands. Both of us knew this was the Hand of Fate!

SIDNEY OWEN

OPERA IN THE HAYFIELD

ONE of the places where I worked while serving in the Land Army in the 1940s was on a big estate with many fields, which were ploughed or planted for food.

During the harvest we had to start work very early, often carrying on until 8pm. I had to cycle a mile to work.

One morning, the farmer told me to harness three horses, and put them in their carts to pick up 10 prisoners-of-war. I was to lead them in the first cart to a distant field nearly half an hour's journey away (I learned that horses never hurry unless they're going home).

Leading a convoy of German prisoners, with nobody else in sight, I was a little apprehensive. How would they react?

I needn't have worried. One who could speak good English asked me if I could sing. He started singing snatches of opera, and I and the rest joined in - me singing with made-up English words!

When we arrived at the field, I had to show the POWs how to load up their carts with hay - one pitching and one in the cart to receive.

I would lead the horse to a pile of hay, then I'd shout "Hold tight" to the men and move to the next pile.

Eventually the foreman put me to helping on the stack. Soon we could hear a loud voice, and looked down. One of the POWs was shouting to the horse: "Hold tight". He began to get cross because the horse wouldn't move - I think he was swearing at it in German.

The foreman let me go and lead for the rest of the day - I was glad because the hay came up the elevator so quickly that as soon as I'd passed it to the 'builder' the next lot nearly buried me. (Many stacks later I learned how to tread it.)

An aunt sent me a cartoon which showed two men on a stack, with just a pitchfork sticking out of it. One of them was saying: "I wonder what happened to little Mary?".

MARY McLELLAND

NEW RECRUIT TO ENSA

I FELT that my posting to Le Bourget Airport, Paris, just after the liberation of the city, must have been some sort of reward.

I had taken part in the D Day landings in Normandy as a radio operator in one of the Royal Air Force Beach Units, and was posted back to France following a spell under canvas in Wiltshire.

Paris had become very much a centre of entertainment for troops on leave, and being a musician as well as a radio operator, I found myself one day being instructed to report to the offices of ENSA in the Champs Elysees.

There I was given an audition and promptly enrolled as pianist for one of the RAF Ralph Reader Gang Shows. I soon found that the rest of the company were all WAAFS.

There were about 12 of them - all gorgeous girls - and I was to be the only male member of the Gang. Even their commanding officer was female, and she was pretty good-looking, too. They were a mixed group of dancers, comediennes and singers of considerable talent.

In spite of all this, I didn't really want to leave Paris, but after a short rehearsal, we were off in a coach bound for Germany, with a small piano and about eight skips of costumes and props.

We gave shows pretty well every night at army and air force camps, and everywhere we went the girls were an enormous success.

Sometimes we worked on a rickety stage made up of wooden boxes, and sometimes we were in a garrison theatre. Sometimes a young officer would come over to me at the piano, and ask if I would give one of the girls a message.

It wasn't easy being one among a group of girls like this, and any male reader will commiserate with me when I say that it sometimes kept me awake at nights. I soon got to know what 'girl talk' was and became quite used to seeing stockings and other things hanging up to dry all over the place.

No female members of the Expeditionary Forces were allowed out without an escort, so in the girls' free time, I was much in demand to go with them on trips to the nearest town.

Towards the end of the tour, we were booked in at a leisure centre in the Black Forest, with heavy snow lying on the pine trees high up in the mountains. I remember climbing up the mountainside in the snow with one of the girls, and drinking ersatz coffee at a kind of chalet.

One day I went for a ski lesson and broke my ankle. I was in quite a bit of pain and I shall always remember the girls' concern for me as they carried me up the slope to an ambulance in the winter sunshine. I had a stay in hospital in Brunswick before being posted back to the UK on crutches.

TONY SAVAGE

JUST
THE JOB

EQUAL TREATMENT

TOWARDS the end of 1941, I volunteered for the ATS, and was called for a medical and job assessment. I was interviewed by an officer and asked what I would like to do. I replied: "Anything but office work!" I was told a new category had just come in - R.Lo.M. The officer did not know exactly what it was, but a high standard of physics and maths was required. I had reached matriculation standard in these subjects, so I was put down for this.

Later I learned that R.Lo.M. meant Radio Location Mechanics. The work was very complicated and highly secret - all our notes had to be locked away each night and extra study had to be done in the workshops in the evenings. We were unable to tell anyone what we were doing.

Towards the end of September 1942, we received our first posting - to RAOC Workshops at Charminster, Dorset. There was no accommodation for women at the camp so a large part of a local house was commandeered for our use.

At the time there were just us nine privates - no NCOs or officers. We were received with mixed feelings by the men in the camp. One of the first jobs they willingly handed over to us was keeping the workshops spick and span. Because of the smallness of some of the items used in the equipment, the benches and floors had to be kept polished and dust-free. We even had to wear felt overshoes in the workshops.

We worked a six-day week, three days from 8am to 6pm, alternating with three days working 8am to 8pm. If we worked late on Friday, we had Saturday free - the next week we worked late Saturday and had Sunday off. This meant that we occupied the workshops until 8pm - or later if there was an emergency - so the cleaning took us until about 10pm.

We dubbed ourselves 'The Charminster Chars', and complained often and loudly, but as the complaints went through the male sergeant they seemed to go no further.

One Friday night at about 9.30pm we were just finishing polishing the floor when the phone rang. One of the girls picked it up and said: "Charminster Chars speaking".

A man's voice said: "This is your CO speaking. You have a crack of light showing in one of your windows… who did you say you were?" "Charminster Chars, sir." She went on to explain our situation, including the fact that our protests were not passed on.

Next day on morning parade, the CO came out and gave the men a lecture. We girls were as much part of the workforce as they were, he said - all jobs such as cleaning and lighting fires were to be done on a strict rota and we were to be treated the same as them in every way.

After that, we went out on site to work, carrying on there until the sites were back in action, regardless of how long it took. We went on route marches with the men, marching in the centre of the columns. At first, the marching songs they sang were very restrained, but soon they forgot we were there, and we learned some entirely new versions.

NORMA MANN

A BLOW TO MORALE

I WAS serving with a minesweeping flotilla in the Royal Naval Patrol Service in 1943, when the CO sent for me. "Oh, Shiers," he said, "I understand you play the fiddle." I replied: "Yes, sir".

"Well, I need a bugler for the ship," he said, "so I'm going to send you back to the depot for a five-day course on the bugle."

Dutifully I journeyed back to the depot. When the five days were up, I rejoined the ship, and speedily realised that as a bugler I was a good fiddle player. How was I to get rid of the job without offending the Old Man?

I decided to practise on the messdeck, the bulkhead of which adjoined the officers' wardroom. Some days elapsed before I was again told to report to the CO.

"Shiers," he said, "I realise you have to practise the bugle, but what I want you to do is take the small boat, row over to the beach, and blow it there."

This I did, much to the disgust of the seagulls. On returning to the ship, I continued practising on the messdeck.

Finally the CO could stand it no longer. "All right, Shiers," he said. "I get the message - you don't want to do the job. I'll get someone else to do it."

C A SHIERS

OPERATION FALSE TEETH

AS A Bevin Boy during the war, picked by lot to go into the mining industry, several funny moments occurred.

One hot summer's evening we were loading props on tubs from the pit head for transportation to the pit bottom.

'Banksman' is the name given to the miner controlling the cages from the surface of the colliery, and on this occasion Frank was in charge, a delightful character with a broad Yorkshire accent. Aged about 60, he had worked at the same pit since leaving school.

We started a fire to burn the odd pieces of wood. Smoke was sucked up in the draught from the cages travelling up and down the shaft. Suddenly a mighty yell came from Frank's direction. We thought he had suffered a heart attack. I rushed over to him. "What's up, Frank - are you all right?"

"Aye," he said angrily. "But the smoke from your bloody fire made me cough and me false teeth have fallen down t'shaft."

"Not to worry, we'll find them, won't we?" I said, turning to Geoff, my Bevin Boy colleague. There was a moment's silence.

"Er, yes," came the reply. "But how?"

We held a short consultation and decided the only way to trace the missing teeth was to go down the shaft strapped on top of the cage with our lamps, looking on all the ledges.

Frank rang up Charlie, who was on duty in the winding room. "It's Operation False Teeth, Charlie," he said. "Take the cage down slow like - we don't want to be missing two Bevin Boys at the end of the shift."

We fastened ourselves to a large belt round the winding coil on top of the cage, and descended into into the darkness.

About half-way down the shaft, Geoff cried "Hold it." Sparkling like a diamond from the glow of our lamps were Frank's precious teeth, cushioned in a layer of coal dust on a ledge. We continued down the shaft and eventually found the other plate, broken in only one place.

The face of that old miner when we reached the surface with the teeth is something I shall always remember. His dusty skin cracked into a gorgeous smile and, rubbing his eyes, he said: "Eee - thanks, lads, thanks a lot".

The next day we were invited round 'to meet wife', as he put it. "These two Bevin Boys saved my false teeth, love." It was the start of a friendship which lasted for the remainder of our service at the colliery. We returned several times to that small terraced house - and all because of the recovery of Frank's false teeth.

I have to add that this sort of act wouldn't be allowed today, but in the war years, as Cole Porter sang, "Heaven knows, anything goes".

PHIL YATES

A NOVICE COOK

WHEN I joined the ATS, I wanted to be a driver and, although I passed the examination, I was too small to reach the controls of the huge lorries. So after the aptitude tests, I was told I was to be an Army cook.

Our tutor had been a chef at a luxury hotel. He was a cheerful Cockney - a laugh a minute - who demonstrated on his own person where the different cuts of meat were. He always insisted that we launder his aprons, caps and white trousers as he said the Army ruined them. It was no trouble washing them but we had no iron, so we used the hot plate in the kitchen.

At last the day came when we were actually allowed to cook something - jam and bread and butter fritters dipped in sweet batter, with Carnation Milk whipped up into a mock cream. The lads seemed to like it.

Then came the day of our examinations. The chef showed us - just once - how to build a brick oven outside on which to cook a three-course meal.

We lit our fires and cooked roast beef dinners. Some ovens collapsed under the heat - I'm glad to say that mine stood the test.

All but one girl passed the exam, and I became a 'First Class Cook' - Army style, that is.

I was posted to Ilkley, Yorkshire, near my home town of Huddersfield. Our cookhouse was in an old theatre and the mess hall was the auditorium.

The whole place was ancient. The stove was backstage, with rafters overhead, and large rats would peep down at us from them. Naturally, we all screamed and ran - the sergeant shouting after us to "Come back at once!"

We cooked for 400 men and officers, with five girls to one sergeant each shift: two for bacon, two for eggs and porridge

ATS cook - Marjorie Fleur Oldfield

and one for the tea. I'll never forget the Scottish soldier who complained about his porridge. He wanted his with salt, not sugar, so we used to set a plate on one side especially for him. If they were kept waiting, the lads were quick to show their irritation by stamping their feet.

Each mealtime an orderly officer would inspect the men's food, accompanied by a sergeant. One day it was a Scottish officer wearing a kilt. His legs were rather thin and, being young enough to be silly, we giggled and were put on a charge.

I still recall the dance we had, and a talent contest where I sang Who's Taking You Home Tonight?. I won, and my prize was to have my photograph taken at the best place in town.

MARJORIE FLEUR OLDFIELD

HEADS I LOSE

WHEN I began my naval service, a petty officer asked for a volunteer to be captain of the heads. This sounded as if it might be a good number, so I volunteered.

The other sailors looked at me with some amusement, and I soon found out why. I should have known better - the job was that of lavatory attendant!

BILL DREW

CITY GIRL
IN THE COUNTRY

I ENROLLED in the Women's Land Army - although I had lived in London all my life, I had loved the country from a very early age and had no fear of animals.

On November 2, 1942, I was sent to Sparsholt Training Farm near Winchester for four weeks of intensive training in dairy and general farm work.

There were six of us from London and we were met at Winchester Station by an open lorry. Other girls came from different parts of the country. We were put into a dormitory with six in each room. Our food rations were a pot of jam to last the month, a small bowl of sugar, and a dish with our ration of butter and margarine to last the week (it never did!) They all had labels with our names.

One week, our butter was rank. After I went to complain to the cook and was given margarine in its place, the rest of the girls went and had theirs changed too.

We used to go into Winchester on our one half-day and buy Marmite (which was not on points or rationed) and anything else we could 'persuade' sympathetic shopkeepers to part with. Our parents sent cakes which we shared with our dormitory. We always seemed to be hungry.

At the end of the four weeks, I was sent to Banbury, where I was taken to an excellent private billet. I was made very welcome and always had plenty to eat. I started at 6am, and was told I was to do a milk round in and around Banbury in the morning and farmwork in the afternoon.

I had a shock when I was told I was to drive a van. I had never driven anything other than a bumper car at the fair, but the farmer said he would soon teach me. The van had defective brakes and no hooter, and I had to drive through Banbury market place on market day! I became known as the Yellow Peril.

One day I had a very heated argument with the police superintendent. I had to deliver milk in the town and leave the van while I went to several customers with two large hand-crates of milk. When I returned to the van, the officer told me I couldn't leave it there.

I told him that if he would carry my crates of milk, I would leave the van wherever he wanted. He eventually left and told me not to stay any longer than necessary.

If our money was short on a Saturday, it was taken out of our meagre wages, but if it was over we never had the extra. I was 10 shillings short one week and could never find out how, but had to lose it in my wages, at five shillings a week.

We paid for our lodgings out of our wages. I was in Banbury for just over a year before I was sent to a farm about seven miles away, which was owned by an old and very eccentric lady. I did not know it until later, but I was to be her 26th land girl, and I stayed with her the longest - one year.

I had to drive this elderly lady into Banbury each week in a large old Austin car, and always had to dress up in my best full uniform. I soon realised why she couldn't keep her land girls and after an unforgettable year, I was transferred to another farm in the nearby village.

This was completely different. I used to work with three huge farm horses, Prince, Bluebird and The Colt. My first job was to fetch them from the field each morning and harness them up. All went well until one morning when I had the halters on Prince and The Colt, but Bluebird wouldn't come. As I stood there holding a horse on each side of me, Bluebird suddenly charged straight at me.

He was about 12 yards away when I threw up my arms and shouted the first thing that came into my head: "Scram!" The enormous animal was so surprised that he skidded to a halt and as I walked the other two down into the village, I let the rebel follow.

When I told the farmer what had happened, he said "Oh, has he started that with you? That's a pity." I asked him why he hadn't told me what Bluebird was like, and he said: "If I'd told you before, you wouldn't have fetched him, would you?"

JOAN CLIFFORD

GUNFIRE?
WHAT GUNFIRE?

I WAS a munitions worker for two years in a factory at Stamford, Lincolnshire, on a constant night shift.

We were a target for night raids and had more than our share of incendiary bombs and flak. When things got a bit too close for comfort we dived under the benches, but normally we were at our posts as long as possible, while our foreman made various excuses for distant - and not too distant - gunfire.

A favourite excuse was "It's a thunderstorm coming up" or "A lot of heavy traffic going by" or "That'll be them emptying the bins".

After one particularly heavy raid, when incendiary bombs were landing on the roof, one wag was heard to remark: "I suppose that will be someone doing the jitterbug on the roof".

MARGARET MORTON

RATS - AND
OTHER PESTS

DURING the war I became a rat catcher in the Women's Land Army. This involved cycling on very heavy bikes, equipped with massive tins of poison, up to 30 miles a day - after we'd cycled to work in the first place. The foreman in charge of the Land Army girls was extremely strict: he had no time for squeamish females and expected us to be as tough as men.

On Mondays and Tuesdays we visited farms in the Harrogate area, putting down bait in rat holes. On Wednesday we 'starved' the rats, and on Thursdays we put poison down - being very careful not to poison anyone, or anything, but rats. On Fridays, we went back to pick up the bodies with our bare hands - the foreman thought gloves were cissy. Finally we dug holes and buried them, or sometimes we burned them. On Wednesdays and on Saturday mornings, we caught moles.

When I worked in the area around Ilkley Moor, the gamekeeper resembled the Mellors character in Lady Chatterley's Lover. While I was working alone with him, he would often mention the wantonness of a 'Lady Penelope' and how she would take off her knickers and trample them in the mud. I didn't respond to this. He also used to extend our lunchtime - particularly if we were near a haystack.

He used to say: "Women'll be the death of me", and hold speedwells up to my eyes, saying they matched. They didn't, of course! However, he was very gentlemanly, brushing the 'cuckoo spit' off the grass before I sat down for lunch.

No-one ever asked Land Girls if they were well - everyone assumed we had such a wonderfully healthy life. The truth was that we were nearly all ill a great deal of the time with various aches, pains and virus infections, owing to the nature of the work and the rough and unhygienic conditions. We were unable to wash our hands during the day and had to use some incredible outdoor 'earth' loos - often, there were no loos at all.

One day some troops marched smartly past another Land Girl and myself and the CO remarked: "How wonderful it must be to feel so well". We felt ghastly.

DRUSILLA WEST

LOTS OF CUDDLES

I WONDER how many people spent their war work dispensing lots of love and cuddles! I was a nursery nurse at the Hillingdon Day Nursery in Middlesex, and although I don't have any exciting tales to tell - it wasn't that kind of work - I do have lots of happy memories.

We cared for 60 youngsters aged from three months to five years old, from 7am to 6pm in a pre-fab building, enabling their mothers to work in the local factories.

The work was a recognised training - with weekly lectures and endless 'practicals' for the National Society of Children's Nurses badge and certificate. This was a great boon - most of us who worked there would never have been able to afford the fees to get the qualification at a training college.

During the day, the babies' feeds were carefully measured out into sterilised bottles and their vegetables sieved - but when Mum came to collect them, they would be propped up in their prams with a handful of chips in front of them on top of the mackintosh pram cover. They would tuck in - all greasy hands and faces, and broad smiles - apparently none the worse for their change in diet!

There were eager open mouths, too, for the daily dose of cod liver oil.

'Potty time' in the Baby Room would see a dozen babies perched on enamel potties - digging their heels into the floor and pulling the potties along at a rate of knots!

JEAN LYNES

The children's Christmas party, 1944, at the Hillingdon Day Nursery, Middlesex.
Jean is holding a baby on the extreme right of the back row.

DODGING
THE RATS AND MICE

OUR day as members of the Women's Land Army in Thorney, Cambridgeshire, started at about 6am.

We had to pack up our own lunch (known as 'dockey' in the Fens), consisting mostly of bread and cheese. On rare occasions we had a hard-boiled egg or a slice of corned beef. Then there was a small slice of cake. We were each given a saucer with a small amount of marg and butter on it, which had to last us a week.

Some girls mixed their marg and butter together - others used either the butter or the marg first, but it was always a job to eke it out.

Breakfast over and our bedding folded neatly on our bunks, we set off to the farm about six miles away, where our first job was potato-picking. It made our backs ache, and we were tired out when we cycled back to the hostel after an eight-hour day. Lunch was eaten out in the fields - no toilet or washing facilities, only a ditch.

Other jobs included sugar beet chopping and carting, and threshing - which we hated as the dust from the corn stack and chaff would get in our eyes, making them red and sore, and would cling to our clothes.

Rats and mice would often fall on us as we worked on the chaff box. Some jobs were more pleasant, such as hoeing in the spring, but the rough, heavy jobs seemed to come along more than the good ones.

When we were carting during harvest time, we were told that we could ride on the horse's back when we had an empty cart, but not when the cart was full. At first, I couldn't see myself riding at any time, but after 'running' to and from the cornfield and knowing that I wouldn't be able to keep it up all day, I decided to brave it and clambered up on the horse's back. Once I got used to it, I really enjoyed working with the huge Suffolk Punch horses.

Carting sugar beet during the winter wasn't as pleasant because we had to work with two cart-horses, one in front of the other, each of them weighing around a ton. The ground would be wet and muddy and we were all slipping and sliding along, so it was rather nerve-racking.

Summertime on the farm wasn't always glorious, either. Sometimes it was too hot to work, but we couldn't stop and sunbathe. The work had to be done.

BETTY SPRIDGEON

NAAFI DAYS

AFTER I left school at 14, I worked for two years in my mother's tea shop, so at 17, I joined the NAAFI when the war came.

My first posting was to a WAAF canteen just over eight miles from home, and I arrived there on my bicycle, with a small suitcase strapped onto the carrier.

I was shown into my billet, and handed bedclothes, a blue overall and a cap, and told to report to the kitchen when I had changed my clothes and made my bed (which had one leg missing and was propped up on a biscuit tin).

I arrived at staff coffee time and while we were getting to know each other, a message came over the tannoy announcing a lecture that night in our canteen.

The manageress and Nellie, the other assistant, laughed and said I would have an easy first night - we'd only need to have a kettle boiling for the bodies.

I didn't ask any questions, and sure enough, a couple of airmen who had passed out during the lecture were brought in to us to be revived.

In my innocence, I sympathised that I didn't like first aid lectures either - I discovered later that the subject had been venereal disease.

Rhoda Woodward - a Cinderella story from the NAAFI

She told me I had to be clean and smart to go out on the bar, and that Nellie always looked smart. My embarrassment turned to anger. I told her I had been working so hard all morning that I hadn't had time to wash and that Nellie had said she was going to clean the billet but she hadn't, so she had had time for a bath. I was fighting back tears and frightened I would be sent home.

Kindly, and that was the only time I ever heard her speak kindly, she asked me to tell her what I had done. "Polished the range, the tea pots and tea urns; kept the fire going, and the boiler; brought in buckets of coal..." - the list went on and on.

Later, Miss Nightmare, as we called her, told me she had spoken to our manageress and that together they had compiled two lists of jobs so that both Nellie and I did a fair share of the work.

RHODA WOODWARD

There was a lot of tough cleaning to be done besides the actual serving of food. We only had scrubbing brushes, soap, Vim and soda. I think it was on my first morning, when I was trying to get everything done and had just about finished, that Nellie, having earlier told me that she was going back to clean the billet, said it was almost time to open the canteen up for break.

I just had time to put on a clean overall and have a quick 'lick and a promise' before the area manager turned up. I can still remember how shamed I felt when she turned over my work-grimed paw and revealed two white 'tidemarks' down my forearm.

SEEING LIFE IN THE ATS

I WAS 18 in 1943, and decided to join the ATS, where living with so many other girls came as a bit of a shock at first.

The child of elderly parents, I had moved to London from Devon in the 1930s. As my father had died and my mother was on her own, I applied for a compassionate posting - and was sent to North Yorkshire! It was June - but the camp, the sea and everything else was bitterly cold.

The inmates of the camp seemed to speak a foreign language, but I managed to pass a couple of trade diplomas, and got a few shillings more. My junior commander and most of the NCOs were very kind to me, but after a few months they realised I was a square peg in a round hole, and I was posted to Maidstone in Kent - not to Nissen huts this time but to a beautiful stately home.

I was interested in my work, which was social welfare, but disturbed by the number of pregnancies I had to deal with. Most of the girls concerned swore they didn't know how it happened! (Mind you, to show how naive I was myself, when someone told me to beware of so-and-so as she was a lesbian, I thought they meant she belonged to a peculiar religion.)

A few times a week we would go into Maidstone to the Star Ballroom, where we had our pick of dance partners - British soldiers and airmen as well as Yanks.

We weren't particularly worried about being so near to Dover and a possible invasion - we knew we were going to win the war.

Although I was officially on a compassionate posting, all leave was stopped and none of us were allowed to leave the area. We soon realised why. One morning we woke to find that virtually every soldier had left in the night. D-Day had begun - and it had been such a well-kept secret that we girls had slept through the evacuation.

BETTY ROEBUCK

HOP PICKERS

THE hop fields of Kent were a welcome change of scene for Londoner Bill Barnes when he came home on leave from the Merchant Navy.

The two pictures, taken in 1946, show him (top) larking around with his brother and sister, and right, with his father and aunt on a hop-picking holiday.

DIRTY WORK
ON THE FARM

I JOINED the Women's Land Army on October 13, 1941, and was posted to Wokingham as a thresher.

Maude Wade and I were billeted with a Mr and Mrs Bird near Wokingham. I had always had my own bed and was horrified to find I had to sleep with Maude in the hardest, lumpiest feather bed I had ever seen. That first night, no matter what we did, we ended in a tangled heap in the middle.

Our employer for threshing was known as Boss - his real name we never knew. His mate, who was also nameless but answered to any grunts from Boss, lived in a dirty, ramshackle caravan.

Boss drove the battered old car which towed the caravan, while Mate trundled behind on the traction engine, pulling the old-fashioned thresher.

Boss collected us each morning at 7am and when we got to work, the traction engine would already be turning the drum of the thresher, accompanied by an ear-splitting whine.

Maude was set up to keep the chaff away from under the machine. I was on top of the machine, armed with a sharp knife to cut the twine round the sheaves as they were pitched up. Then I had to push the loosened sheaf down into the drum. It was noisy, dirty and dangerous work, with the possibility of slipping on loose straw and falling into the unguarded drum.

Near the end of the second week, Boss told Maude he did not want her any more but that I could stay. He said he would not call for me each day and I was to live with the two men in the caravan. That's what he thought!

Next morning, Maude and I went to our regional office at Reading. We collected a black mark against our names for not working, were lectured, and sent back to

our billet to await events. This was the only time I ever went on strike.

After a year I was transferred to Fawkham in Kent. One morning, Brenda Lane and I were detailed to go to the potato clamp to riddle a ton of potatoes and sack them up into bags for market. On the way, we suddenly realised a plane was apparently dive-bombing us.

We leapt straight into a very muddy ditch and prayed the bomb would miss us. The plane flew on, and we rose, shaken and filthy, to find a jettisoned auxiliary fuel tank. The pilot must have seen us and laughed himself silly all the way back to the aerodrome.

Later I was transferred to Queen Mary Hospital at Sidcup to work in the grounds.

Our biggest nightmare was the pigs we kept. Scraps and uneaten food from the hospital were put into very large bins where, in hot weather, huge colonies of big, white, fat grubs appeared.

All the scraps were tipped into a bath, the cover put on, and it was steamed. This delectable offering was wheeled up to the two pig paddocks.

One very hot day, I was in the paddock taking the full buckets and dutifully pouring it into the trough for the just-weaned piglets.

One got into the trough, treading the mess, and to get him out, I smacked his little curly tail. He squealed, popped his front trotters over the edge of the trough, and scooped a very large dollop of hot, smelly pig food out.

For a small pig, his aim was perfect - the mess went straight into my face, then slowly trickled down inside my open-necked shirt and proceeded to my knees. I was banished to the bathroom the moment I got home.

O F CRANE

Above: Madeleine Croll

TYPING FOR ENGLAND

IN 1942, the WAAF and WRNS were recruiting balloon barrage crews and cooks.

Weighing just seven stone six pounds, I could not envisage holding onto a balloon and I was certainly no cook.

The last option was the ATS, and I joined as a shorthand-typist (120 wpm and 65 wpm respectively).

After training camp in Devon, I was sent to the ATS clerks' school in Strathpeffer, Scotland, where the intake was told they would emerge doing 50 wpm shorthand.

This caused some consternation to the commanding officer, when she learned we were all highly qualified to start with.

After instructions from the War Office, we undertook a staff training course with a pass at the end of it that would enable us to work for high-ranking officers.

My pass earned me a posting to a company office in Woking where I never saw a junior officer, let alone a senior one.

"Another one from the clerks' school who can't type," sneered the male sergeant when I arrived, so ignoring him I put some paper in the typewriter and rattled away. His eyes popped out like organ stops.

Eventually I did work for five officers, though not one of them was over the rank of captain.

Surprisingly, we won the war.

MADELEINE CROLL

Left: Peter Daniels, pictured when he was discharged from the Army in 1945

AN EXCELLENT MEAT PUDDING

I TRANSFERRED to the Army Catering Corps after originally being drafted into the Royal Artillery as a gunner in 1940.

I found myself working as cook in the officers' mess when, one day, the colonel summoned all personnel to gas drill.

When the gas alert was called, my gas-cape failed to open and I was told I'd have to have special daily gas-drill until I was proficient at it.

That particular day, I'd made a meat pudding for lunch and as I was taking it from the stove, I accidentally dropped it among the cinders.

Quick as I could, I retrieved it and sent it into the dining room, keeping my fingers crossed!

To my amazement, the colonel sent me a message saying that even if I couldn't do my gas drill, I could certainly make an excellent meat pudding - and I could forget the extra gas drills!

"What the eye doesn't see," I thought…

PETER DANIELS

COUNTRY LIFE

MY first posting in the Women's Land Army was to a hostel for 12 girls at Bourn, a village about eight miles from Cambridge.

We were sent out to do seasonal work on various farms, often working alongside Italian POWs, conscientious objectors, and once, a refugee from Europe.

31

Work could be hoeing, picking and plating potatoes; harvesting or clearing land for the planting of new crops. We could also do tractor work and use threshing or baling machines. Some jobs lasted only a few days - others, like land clearing - might last for weeks.

We were paid 1s per hour, so we received £2 4s weekly. Of this, £1 1s went to pay for our keep at the hostel. I put 3s aside each week so that I had 12s once a month to pay for a return ticket to London.

That left me with £1 a week for all other expenses, including toiletries and trips to the cinema in Cambridge.

Since we had to work four hours on Saturdays until noon, I worked one hour extra each week so that once a month I could get Saturday off for my visit home.

I would get the War Ag lorry to take me into Cambridge to catch the train for London, returning on Sunday afternoon in time to get the last bus from Cambridge out to Bourn.

In the winter, one sat in the train in darkness unless the compartment had blinds - then there was a light on, its bulb painted blue. I remember going back to Cambridge one freezing winter's day with ice on the inside of the windows.

We were issued with two free passes a year to go home - but they could not be used at Christmas as the trains had to be available for service personnel going on leave.

We were given vacuum flasks for tea at work - I used to wrap mine in scarves to prevent the glass getting broken. Although the glass did not break, the milk in the tea got so shaken up on my bike ride to work over bumpy tracks that it curdled - so I gave up taking a flask of tea and took water in a lemonade bottle.

We all had a little glass screw-top jar for our week's sugar ration - about 2oz each. Since I didn't use mine on porridge or cornflakes, I thought I would get used to drinking tea without sugar. I have never

taken sugar in my tea since.

The family used to bottle fruit and vegetables in Kilner jars, so when I went home I would also try to take them some fresh fruit or vegetables bought locally.

At harvest time, we could get extra rations - 4oz cheese, 4oz margarine and a jar of jam - for our meals out in the fields, when work went on until late evening. The rate for overtime was one penny-halfpenny extra per hour.

JOAN THOMPSON

THE DREADED HOT-ACHES

AT 8am on a grey winter's morning, a field of Brussels sprouts is about as cheerful as a cemetery. The Land Army dungarees and milking coats we wore for jobs around the farm were not all that warm, even worn with green woollen jumpers and knee-length socks.

We had to pick the sprouts off from the bottom of the stalks, working upwards, and put them in nets. We soon found that frozen sprouts were a very icy harvest!

Six of us lived in our hostel, and while we were still warm from our bike ride to work, things were tolerable, but we soon cooled down.

After 20 minutes, we were chilled to the bone and had to break off from work for a chorus of Knees Up Mother Brown, prancing about to get warm as our breath spiralled on the frosty air.

Half an hour later, the sun started to break through, but this added to our troubles.

While the sprouts were hard and frosty, it was easier to pick them off, but as they started to melt, the wetness soaked our gloves and numbed our fingers.

They felt stiff and useless until the

dreaded hot-aches set in as the blood returned. It was agonisingly painful, but there was nothing for it but to press on regardless until our fingers started tingling and normality returned.

At 10.15am we would hear the hum of an approaching tractor as the farmer arrived with cups and a jug of hot tea.

He loaded our nets of sprouts on his tractor and drove off, leaving us gulping the tea down gratefully and deciding that in future we would look at a dish of Brussels sprouts with more respect!

DOROTHEA ABBOTT

PREPARING FOR WAR

Mr A H W Hayes (centre, back row) sent this photograph of himself and comrades at a Territorial Army camp at Aldershot at Whitsuntide, 1939. He was later captured by the Germans and taken prisoner-of-war.

GEARED UP FOR WAR

THE RUNAWAY VAN

I WAS a member of the Women's Land Army in Wales, where I was taught to drive a Ford van in three weeks. I delivered milk near Caernafon.

One day on my way back to the farm, I wasn't happy with the steering. I stopped and looked at all the tyres, thinking that I might have a puncture. I could see nothing wrong, so I drove on.

Arriving at the farm, I opened the gate, drove through - and the back wheel fell off!

On another occasion, I parked facing downhill and set off to deliver the milk. Something made me look round - and I saw the van slowly moving off down the hill without me! I dropped the milk can and dashing after the van, managed to get in and stop it. The brakes had failed!

This happened quite early into my round, so for the rest of the day I carried a huge stone with me to put in front of a wheel if I had to park on a hill.

MARION EYRE

AN ILLUMINATING EXPERIENCE

I HAD an uncanny experience as an air raid warden during the strictly-enforced wartime blackout. As I came on duty one night, I looked up and saw the brilliantly-

lit window of our rooftop fire-watchers' hut shining like a beacon from the top of an office block.

I ran up the stairs, determined to catch whoever was responsible, only to find the place empty and in darkness. But when I got back down to street level again, I looked up and the light was still blazing.

When this had happened twice, I felt more apprehensive than bewildered. Was some enemy agent signalling a flight path for a bombing raid?

I climbed up to the roof for the third time, threw open the hut door - and again, encountered total darkness. Summoning all my courage, I flashed my torch around the hut, drew the curtains and slammed the door - and immediately the place lit up.

Suddenly I realised that there was a simple explanation. The hut door had a trigger switch which put out the light as anyone left the hut, and lit it again when the door was closed.

The previous firewatchers had opened the black-out curtains in the morning and forgotten to switch the light off.

ARTHUR BROWN

FOILED BY A FOLDING BIKE

THE 156 Parachute Battalion, together with other units of the 1st Airborne Division, were going to take part in an exercise intended to prepare people for the forthcoming invasion of Europe. Somewhere in the upper reaches of higher command, someone decided that I was going to be issued with a folding bicycle.

I must admit to a certain lack of enthusiasm. I eventually unfolded the thing and tried a practice ride, but found this machine to be without merit. It had a fixed wheel, which meant that one could not rest from pedalling when travelling downhill. I began to harbour doubts as to its ability to seriously influence the outcome of an encounter with the enemy.

Nevertheless, I realised that those in authority would sleep easier in their beds if they could truthfully say: "I know our chaps don't have tanks but at least we have supplied them with a rattling good folding bike".

Eventually, the day came for the exercise. I had folded my bicycle in the approved manner and placed it carefully by the door of the Dakota. It had its own parachute and static line so, in theory, all I would have to do, when the time came, was push it out of the plane and follow it.

Our arrival over the dropping zone was relatively uneventful - apart from the container of ammunition we inadvertently released over a West Country town because someone was wriggling about.

The jump light went on, but I made the mistake of attempting to get my bike to go out sideways. It refused. After some pushing and shoving, accompanied by a show of impatience by those behind me, it went and I followed it.

When I arrived on the ground, I collected my equipment from the kit bag and began looking for the bike. It was nowhere to be seen.

Eventually, I chanced to look up. Floating serenely on a gentle breeze - and, moreover, going in the opposite direction to the entire battalion - was my bike. It didn't appear to have descended at all from the height it had reached when I pushed it out of the plane. It was obvious that as I was prevented by the law of gravity from rejoining my bicycle, I would have to wait until it joined me.

Eventually it arrived, but not before the battalion had disappeared over the horizon.

I hastily unfolded the machine and attempted to ride it. My forebodings about its suitability as transport for a fully equipped soldier were confirmed. It was useless.

After about half an hour I caught up with my company, who were gathered at the roadside brewing up. I immediately realised that this meant that they were 'dead'. (It was the practice on tactical exercises for 'umpires' to suddenly spring out from the undergrowth and tell units that they had been killed and would come back to life two hours later.) During 'death' they could stop and eat.

I realised that, as the only surviving member of the unit, I was to be denied the pleasure of brewing up, but as time passed I became tempted. Surely, I thought, no Army umpire is likely to remember how many soldiers he has temporarily banished - but I was wrong. No sooner had I extracted the solid block of black 'tea' from my haversack, than the umpire sprang from the bushes.

"Soldier," he said. "I don't remember killing you. Why are you brewing up?"

I realised my reply would have to be carefully worded if I wished to continue my brew in peace.

"Well, sir,' I said, "when I managed to retrieve my folding bicycle and rejoin my comrades, I discovered that they had all been killed and I was so overcome by grief at the fate of such a fine body of men that I shot myself."

The umpire's face softened into a smile.

"You're a cheeky young . . ., aren't you?" he said. "OK. You can come back to life with the others".

C B ELLIOTT

NORTH OF THE BORDER

In 1942-43, 931 Company Royal Engineers was stationed at Cairn Ryan, near Stranraer, Scotland.

These pictures, sent by J Darwen, show them going on guard duty (left), building a jetty (below) and being photographed with the camp's cook (below left).

Mr Darwen is the figure on the right of the top picture, and arrowed on the photos below.

DON'T DO AS I DO...

IT was January, 1944, and we were about three weeks into our training at a Fleet Air Arm training camp at Leigh in Lancashire.

About thirty recruits sat in silence during a lecture on the 303 rifle. The Chief Petty Officer explained its intricacies, taking it to pieces and reassembling it as we watched.

Towards the close of the lecture, he warned us: "Always treat your rifle with respect as your life might depend on it - and always check that it is unloaded".

With the rifle butt resting downward on the desk and the barrel pointing up towards the ceiling, the Chief pulled the trigger.

Guess what - there was still a live round in it! There was a terrific bang and a very large hole appeared in the ceiling.

Never have so many recruits moved so fast - mostly under desks. We were quickly dismissed and we heard no more about the incident.

JACK HEARN

THEN AND NOW

AT FIRST glance, the two photographs (below centre and far left) look similar, and so they are. The vehicles are almost identical and the person in the pictures is the same - but they were taken over 50 years apart.

I was given the opportunity to drive an American armoured half-track truck (far left) owned by Richard Cross of Hartwell, and what memories it brought back.

Just after the D Day landings, I was shipped over to France as driver of a half-track as part of our unit, 14 Field Squadron - Royal Engineers. We were attached to the Guards Armoured Division and travelled through France, Belgium, Holland and Germany.

Our job was to go ahead lifting mines - building bridges and generally clearing the roads to keep the troops moving. The truck was virtually home for six or seven men. It was filled to over-flowing even on the roof, with our kit and ammunition, plus a box of eggs and a side of bacon, gratefully supplied by the farms we liberated.

Whenever we were able to stop for a few hours, we would cook a good fry-up, a welcome change from the tinned meat and veg supplied by the Army.

Explosives were stored in lockers under the truck. When there was heavy shelling, I often took cover underneath my truck, yet I felt as safe as houses.

DON FARRAND

Don Farrand (left) and fourth from the left, back row, in the group picture

39

SEEING THE WORLD

INSIDE INFLUENCE

IN the summer of 1939, I was just sixteen - fed up with my job, and tired of hearing the adults around me constantly predicting the start of a second world war before the end of the year.

One Sunday morning, I was chatting with a neighbour and was intrigued to learn that his son was second steward on the P&O liner Strathaird.

"He'll be coming home in a few days," our neighbour assured me. "Have a word with him - he'll tell you all about life in the merchant service."

I couldn't wait for Stan to get home. The merchant service! Oh boy! It sounded like one big adventure - living and working aboard a big ocean liner. I'd never been any farther than across the Thames on a paddle steamer.

Several days later I arrived home from my job at a local greengrocer's to hear that Stan was at home and expecting me to call on him.

Although I knew my mother was worried about my leaving the family when the international situation was looking more and more desperate, I also knew that she wouldn't stand in my way if I decided to go.

The glossy picture that Stan painted of life on board ship was, on reflection, no more than one would expect from an experienced seaman who had spent the major part of his life at sea.

Nevertheless, I was sold on the idea. An interview at the shipping company's offices in Tilbury was soon arranged, and eventually I was ordered to report to the officer-in-charge of the shore staff for training.

After a couple of weeks' tuition in my duties as a bell-boy, I was told to report on board the liner Stratheden for a voyage to Australia. The ship sailed from Tilbury on September 1, 1939, with several hundred passengers.

Once clear of the docks, the crew of the purser's department - which included me - was ordered to muster on the boat deck for inspection by the Chief Officer. Passing along the ranks, he stopped and faced me.

"Can you swim, lad?" the Chief Officer asked.

"No, sir," I replied.

"Can you row, then?"

"No, sir."

"Well, could you sail a boat?"

"I don't think so, sir," I answered quietly.

Turning to his subordinate officers, he screamed: "What the hell is this boy doing on this ship?"

I later discovered that all the other lads had spent at least six months at the Gravesend Sea School, training for enrolment in the merchant service.

'Is inside influence a good thing?' I asked myself.

FRED CAREY

A MESSAGE FROM ADOLF

IT was the winter of 1944 and I was a young infantry soldier serving in a Scottish regiment.

The British Army had swept across Europe and airborne troops had tried and failed to take Arnhem in Holland. They had been forced to retreat to Nijmegen, which is where I found myself one clear, crisp evening, out with a patrol in the Dutch countryside.

There was a lull in the fighting, and all was quiet as we trudged through the snow, keeping a wary eye open for German patrols.

As we reached a clearing in the woods, we heard the whoosh of a couple of shells - but no explosion, which was most unusual. A minute later, as propaganda leaflets fluttered down, we learned the reason why.

I picked one up off the snowy ground. As it was a clear night, I was able to read it by moonlight.

On one side was a coloured picture of a scantily-clad female being embraced by a

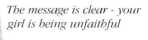

The message is clear - your girl is being unfaithful

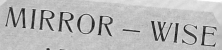

MIRROR – WISE

A Precarious Story

Joan was in her room and just about to change because she intended to go to the Cinema with Bob. She had done that quite often since John, her husband had left for the front. — Why shouldn't she? Bob is a good friend of John's and he certainly wouldn't object. Everybody understands that Joan cannot always sit at home alone for years, without any companionship. —

Yesterday Bob came a little earlier than usual and entered Joan's room just as she was adding the last touch of rouge. She didn't mind his staying for they were really good friends — and so accustomed to each other.

As she rolled on her stockings, Bob told her all that he had done during business hours that day — and then she noticed that the elbow of his jacket had a little grease spot; so she took it and cleaned it. — What could anybody think wrong about that — among friends.

And then — — — Neither knew how it happened, she felt his strong body leaning gently against her — and then — they kissed — for a long — long while.

Joan was in a dream — — — she was feeling that marvellous something that she had missed for so long — it was so wonderful. Then she opened her eyes — and there was that horror before her. Was it a dream — or was it reality?

She looked in the mirror and saw . . . . . . John! John in the arms of another! In the arms of Death!

But no, it was not John embraced by Death — — — it was YOU — and it was not Joan looking in the mirror but YOUR wife.

Joan is still alone.

And so are all the millions of other wives and girls.

But war goes on.

handsome man in evening dress. They were standing in front of a mirror. Reflected in it was a British soldier in the embrace of Death, personified by a skeleton.

The message on the back of the sheet was headed Mirror-Wise: A Precarious Story. The piece of propaganda which followed was aimed at putting into the minds of British soldiers that while they were away fighting for their country, their wives and sweethearts were being unfaithful.

This was all very cunning, but the morale of British troops at that time was such that they merely laughed at the crude attempt to depress them. In fact,

they appreciated the picture of the scantily-clad girl, as pin-ups were much in demand.

A few weeks later we were across the Rhine and the same airborne troops who had been pushed out of Arnhem were now racing through Germany. The end of the war was near.

Fifty-four years later, I still have that leaflet. It is now yellow with age, but it takes me back to the night I received a message from Adolf Hitler in a snowy Dutch wood.

ALLAN WARBURTON

THE WRONG SORT OF TINS

LES and his mate were in the RAF during the war and volunteers were requested for various jobs about the camp. "Don't volunteer to do the spuds," Les told his mate.

Then they heard men were required for 'tin-room' duties. "We'll do that," said Les, "then we'll be able to help ourselves to Spam and fruit when we open the tins".

Imagine their surprise when, instead of helping the cook by opening the tinned food, they found themselves up to the elbows in a sink full of greasy water and baking tins thick with burnt-on food.

JOYCE BROWN

TOWARDS THE SUEZ CANAL

Pages from the 1945 diary of W J Ford, bound for India on the troop ship MV Tegelberg:

Thursday, April 26, 1945:
Pay day today, and we are to have all our money changed into Egyptian currency, so apparently we are going to be in Egypt for some time. We have caught the leading ship of the convoy, which didn't turn into Gibraltar Harbour. We expect to be in Port Said or Suez tomorrow evening or Saturday morning. It is quite fresh today and windy.

Passed the two-funnelled ship which started off from the Clyde River with us. Played housey-housey, but no luck. Bright moonlight night. Still cold. Slipped on the galley deck and had a nasty shake. Hurt my knee and shoulder. Had a dressing applied. Blackout 8.30pm.

Friday, April 27:
Marie's birthday. Reported sick. Had my knee punctured and fluid extracted. My shoulder is better but I am excused duties for three days. Everybody is busy with the disembarking programme.

It's been a nice day but windy. We all changed into khaki drill ready to move off the ship. Had to give up my job today on account of not being able to carry things up and down stairs. Water is scarce now. The water of the Med is a lovely blue today. Flying fish are plentiful.

Saw a dog on board for the first time. Sing-song on board and housey-housey - at the same time. It was one against the other!

Saturday, April 28:
At a standstill when we awoke this morning. After breakfast we dropped anchor at Port Said. From where I stood I could see the entrance to the Suez Canal and the leading ship of our convoy was just going through to India. I saw a child on board her, the first I had seen since leaving Mytchett. Palms are waving on both sides of us.

We are pulled in alongside huge oil tanks. We passed several masts of wrecks in the harbour, probably evidence of dive bombing. There is sand everywhere. All my kit is ready to go ashore - we have had no orders as to the time we go ashore, or even if we have to go. My leg will not allow me to march far anyway.

All rumours have been scotched as all going ashore have gone, and we have had our English money returned. Our kits have been stored away and the ship is taking on provisions, so we are still tied up at the entrance to the Suez Canal. Coolies are plying their wares - cheap jewellery and wallets, but we are warned against buying them. A couple of boys have been in the water diving for pennies.

Port Said looks to be a large place with tall buildings. I expect our next stop to be Bombay. I am hoping we stay here until daylight tomorrow as I think that going through the Canal will be quite thrilling. Playing housey-housey tonight.

W J FORD

SECOND FIDDLE

VIOLIN teacher Gwendolen Marchment whistled through her teeth at my attempts to reach the fifth position on the school-issue Chinese 'Lark' violin.

"I can't teach you any more on that fiddle, William," she sighed. I had to agree - but on my earnings as an engineering apprentice, I couldn't afford a decent instrument.

Gwen produced my second fiddle a week later. "Tyrolean," she explained. "About a hundred years old. £10 - pay me weekly."

The new fiddle helped. Despite the Luftwaffe's daily 'nuisance' raids I took grade four exams at Greenwich Music Academy in London's 'Bomb Alley'. "Don't think they'll come over today," sniffed my examiner. "Too low a cloudbase."

He was wrong. Halfway through a Beethoven piece, we heard roaring Messerschmitt engines and the whistle of falling bombs. Scrambling out from under the piano, I found my fiddle's belly badly gashed. Uncle Jack was a carpenter and repaired the fiddle, but I noticed afterwards that the neck was askew.

I had now joined the Gravesend String Orchestra, gaining valuable sight-reading experience as well as falling for the doctor's daughter who sat next to me. Before I could consolidate this acquaintance, my RAF calling-up papers arrived.

A temporary posting took me to a Suffolk bomber airfield where I was able to use a hangar for practice. One evening a pretty WAAF came in. We got chatting, I put the fiddle on a chair - and then sat on it as the girl bade me goodbye…

Although light to handle and seemingly fragile, a violin is constructed, like a suspension bridge, to withstand enormous pressure. Fortunately, only the bridge was damaged, which I promptly replaced.

The fiddle was looking quite dilapidated now with its scarred belly, twisted

Above: William Topping practising on his well-travelled violin at Tambaram Airfield, Madras, in 1946
Right: in uniform

neck, and an ill-fitting bridge.

At Sudbury, I teamed up with a pianist and we played light music in the officers' mess. The CO's Great Dane Max always started howling when we began to play.

After leaving Sudbury for further training I was posted to India. Should I take the fiddle? One of the 'ex-pat' members of the Gravesend Orchestra warned me that his cello had melted in West Africa in the Twenties. But I decided to chance it.

We left Tilbury in the spring of 1946 on the troopship Strathaird. Reaching Gibraltar, the Strathaird promptly lost its anchor down a bombhole in the harbour. "Two-week's delay for repairs to our

there, south on a week-long rail journey to Madras. I padlocked the fiddle to a luggage rack. At one stop, monkeys climbed in and almost managed to release the padlock!

Tambaram airfield outside Madras provided an opportunity to practise for the grade six exams daily. Early mornings, playing completely naked, were best to avoid the heat.

At the start of the monsoons I had to travel to Ootacamund in the Nilgiri mountains to collect some aircraft instruments. 'Ooty' was cool enough for evening log fires.

Back at Tambaram I went straight to the fiddle and lifted it out. Only the fingerboard came away! The monsoon's humidity had softened the glued joints. My violin lay in pieces.

The Musee Musicale shop in Madras tut-tutted: "We have many European stringed instruments in like this: we refix them with tropical glue."

One week later, I was posted to Calcutta. I had to retrieve the fiddle first. "It is still in cramps," protested the Musee Musicale.

With the cramps it was like a small cello. An oversize kitbag just contained it. I dismantled my Sten gun, stuffed it into the violin case, and staggered onto the Calcutta train. There we learned we would be going to Singapore by Sunderland flying boat: our luggage (including my fiddle) would go by sea!

When we got to Singapore docks a week later, our kit was being unloaded by crane-and-net, cascading onto the dockside. Astonishingly, the fiddle survived. Its belly was distorted and the soundpost cracked, but I played it afterwards in the Singapore Orchestra.

Two years later I returned home. My music teacher stared aghast at the battered fiddle. "What on earth happened?" she said.

I took a deep breath: "Well, it was like this…"

WILLIAM TOPPING

anchor," bellowed the tannoy. "Shore leave will be arranged." Everybody cheered. Two weeks holiday in Gib!

A scratch band was wanted for the Rock's service clubs, so I joined. We played all types of stuff, from the pop tunes of the day to light classics. Free drink abounded: one evening red wine was tipped over my fiddle. It sounded strangled, and changed to a muddy red colour. "Looks like a proper Strad now, mate," said our trumpeter.

We reached Port Said before entering the Suez Canal. As the Strathaird sailed out into the sweltering Red Sea, I took the precaution of slackening the fiddle strings.

At Bombay we were immediately dispatched to scorching Delhi, and from

SAILOR IN TRAINING

AS a boy at a small village school in Hampshire, I had one burning ambition - to travel and see the world. The problem was: how?

The obvious answer was to go to sea, so I wrote to the nearest Royal Navy recruiting office, only to be told that they did not accept boys under the age of 15. I was 14. But they sent a list of training ships that might accommodate me.

I wrote to some of them and was finally offered a place on the Arethusa, a four-masted ship moored in the River Medway opposite the naval dockyard of Chatham.

I stepped aboard to become a sailor. The date was June 26, 1936 - a date I will never forget. The first thing we had to do was to hand over all our pocket money, which was then doled out once a week at the rate of 4d each.

We were told that after six months of good conduct, the ship would pay us 2d per week, which took the pressure off our meagre savings. After 12 months, we would get 4d a week. I had come to a strange new world of commands, disciplines, and punishments.

Smoking was strictly forbidden and anyone caught doing so was immediately taken down to the gym, told to put on a pair of thin cotton trousers, bent over a vaulting horse and given three to six strokes of the cane, according to the whim of the officer in charge. Boys who ran away and were caught - which they all were - had a stiffer sentence.

Boys talking in the ranks were sent over the 170-foot foremast in bare feet - not a pleasant or an easy experience in the winter, when the rigging was covered in ice.

Boots were issued, but were only worn

Above: Harry Jeffery, photographed at the outbreak of war in 1939

THE DUNKIRK SPIRIT

OUR gun was in position on Messines Ridge, Belgium, in 1940, when the order came through: "Pack up - we're heading for Dunkirk".

"Which Dunkirk?" queried Dusty Miller. "The one in Scotland?"

"There's one in Kent," I said. "I could get home from there."

"I reckon it's the one in France," said Bill Goodall. "Blimey, I hope it is - there's a smashing beach."

HARRY JEFFERY

at Sunday divisions or on shore leave, which was not very often.

There was also a set of unwritten laws. The first of these was that new boys sat at the bottom of the mess table (which seated 12) and they received the smallest portions.

On washdays, the older boys had first share of the wash tub to do their laundry. The younger ones had to use the dirtier water. New boys were dumped in the tub to initiate them. After the clothes were washed and hung out on the upper deck, we used the water to wash down the maindeck, scrubbing it on our hands and knees. It was then that I found out what housemaid's knee meant.

Lights out was at 9pm, when we turned into our hammocks. If you were slow, you had your bare legs lashed with a cane. There was one officer who seemed to get a lot of pleasure out of that. The bugle aroused us at 6am to lash and stow our hammocks, get a cold water wash and then dash up to the upper deck to muster, egged on by an officer at the foot of the ladder with a rope end in his hand.

After muster, it was down to breakfast where we had a slice of bread, a spoonful of jam and a mug of stuff called cocoa. On Sundays we each had a small hard-boiled egg.

After just over 12 months of this, I was drafted to Shotley Barracks, to the notorious HMS Ganges near Harwich, where the treatment was supposed to be really rough and tough.

Coming from a training ship, I found it not too bad. More to the point, we now received one shilling and sixpence pocket money - which, of course, we spent on food in the NAAFI.

After 15 months or so at Shotley as a signals boy, I went to sea little realising what lay ahead of me. That was to be six years of the Battle of the Atlantic. Unlike dozens of my training ship friends, I was lucky to come out of it alive.

RON HAYES

AN EASY LIFE

FOR the last part of my army life I was stationed in Italy. Like most units, we had a sergeant-major and a very strict one.

I fell ill with jaundice and was sent to hospital. When I recovered, I returned to my unit, and reported to the orderly room, where I was told to report to our sergeant-major.

"Can you ride a motor-bike?" he asked. "Yes, sir," I said. He gave me a chit to draw a bike from the compound, and when I reported back to him with it, handed me a sealed dispatch bag and told me to take it to HQ.

What an easy number, I thought. A nice ride out to the other side of Naples, wait for dispatches to be taken, and wait to be given another sealed bag to take back!

One morning, as I stood to attention in his office, he showed me a long narrow box. "There's too much fiddling," he said. "So I've had this box made with cards in. Everybody is on the list, so nobody can get off doing guard duty."

It soon dawned on me that when my name was getting near the front of the box, all I had to do was put my card to the back! It worked - I never did guard duty any more.

N CRAVEN

A PROTEST ON THE EMPIRE WOODLARK

THIS is the story of a difference of opinion between the top brass and the troops. I joined the RAF on my 18th birthday in November, 1940, and applied for service overseas early in 1942. On June 20 that year, I sailed off down the Mersey on the 17,000-ton Empress of Russia, built in 1913.

After a three-day stop in Freetown, West Africa, our convoy reached Durban, South

Africa, where we were welcomed by The Woman in White, who sang patriotic songs to us while her helpers distributed fresh fruit. We were loaded onto a troop train which took us to the transit camp at Clairwood, just outside Durban.

After a couple of weeks, it became a regular thing to visit the docks to see if another convoy had arrived. We knew it would probably mean the next stage of the journey to our undisclosed destination.

One day late in July, we were suddenly summoned to pack up and prepare to move out. This came as a surprise as we had not seen any ships of significant size in the docks the previous day.

Our troop train, heavily laden with men from all three services, was confronted at the dockside halt by what appeared to be a filthy tramp steamer. This was the Empire Woodlark, built in 1913 - as its name had the prefix 'Empire', we knew it was a captured (or acquired) enemy ship. I now know it was formerly the Emma Alexandra.

We were directed to the mess decks, which were dirtier than the exterior. My particular sweathole had a thriving colony of bugs and cockroaches.

By this time I felt hot and dirty so I thought I'd take a shower as it would be my last chance to use the piped water from the dockside. When I returned, I found the mess deck empty, but I could hear loud voices from above.

I joined a crowd making their way onto the open deck and to my amazement, saw men from all three services going down the gangway onto the dockside, shouting protests about the bad conditions. The exodus continued during the afternoon and into the night. By this time I was also 'over the side' as there seemed little point in being lonely on a bug-infested empty mess deck.

We were addressed and threatened by senior officers - one of whom appeared to have had a tincture or two.

Next morning, before the dock workers were up and about, we were returned to Clairwood, and confined to camp, apart from some route marches. After a couple of weeks, restrictions were lifted.

Some weeks later we were again taken to the docks - to a much improved model of troop ship, the Orient Line's Oronsay. Once again, we did not know our destination but we didn't mind as conditions were very good.

Imagine our horror when we heard the ship was heading for the UK. I had visions of courts martial and glass-houses. But after three or four days at sea, the ship put in at Capetown, where we disembarked. We were immediately put onto the 20,000-ton Dominion Monarch, built in 1939, which was fast, well-stocked and decently accommodating.

My service records show I disembarked in Bombay on October 18, 1942. I suppose that, thanks to the Empire Woodlark, our voyage must have set some sort of record for the longest time to get from the UK to India.

● As for the Empire Woodlark, her end, to my mind, was fitting. Some time in 1946, she was loaded up with unwanted war material, taken out to sea, and scuttled.

MICK MINE

48

TRAVELS WITH A CANARY

I WAS with the Blue Funnel Line on the Far East run in World War II. I remember playing cricket in Shanghai, buying a canary and cage for the equivalent of 40p in Hong Kong, and falling in love with a girl called Leonie in Singapore.

I was stranded in Gibraltar for a month, waiting to join a convoy for home at Christmas time.

I eventually reached Liverpool in midwinter. It was snowing hard, and I was carrying a canary in a cage. I got a few strange glances on the tram in Manchester.

In those days, the crew got their leave while the ship went 'coasting' - delivering the cargo brought from the East.

I was listening to the radio one evening when the news came on and I heard that my ship had struck a magnetic mine off the Welsh coast. There were no more details in case Lord Haw-Haw was listening.

That canary was a survivor. He lived a few more years until one day he fell off his perch into the sugar bowl.

STAN ALLMAN

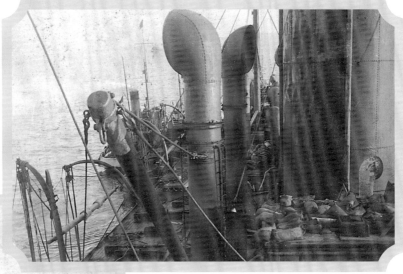

Above: The beaching of the ship Stan served on
Left: The photograph of the Singapore river and the Supreme Court that Leonie sent Stan as a memento

SEEING INDIA - BY RAIL

AT the age of 16, I was serving in India as a band boy in the Regimental Band of the South Staffordshire Regiment. Even at that young age I had seen the Suez Canal. However, in 1936 I was to experience an event more memorable than any other in my life - a train journey that took eight days and nights.

At the crack of dawn we marched from Baird Barracks, each person carrying his webbing, equipment and full backpack to the city station at Bangalore in Southern India to catch the train to Cawnpore, in the north of the country.

There were six people to a carriage, with little room to move and no padded seats. We were bothered by flies and mosquitoes - not to mention the intolerable heat - and this was to be our home for eight long days and nights.

If we wanted to brew a cuppa, we had to wait until the train had stopped, and then rush along to the engine with a can to get boiling water. We had been forbidden to drink the soft drinks peddled by Indian vendors.

Each day at about noon, we would stop at some remote station, get off the train, and march off to nowhere and back for exercise while the battalion cooks tried to concoct a hot meal.

The cooks were untrained - the catering corps had not then been formed. I still believe their toad in the hole was made with real toads and that the meat they used came from the local boot repairers!

There was only one small toilet, shared by about 40 of us, which was only to be used when the train was moving. Every time it stopped there was a mad rush for the nearby bushes. Imagine the chaos during the hours of darkness.

We were into the second half of our long journey when someone who was reading an Indian newspaper informed us

that the temperature in Cawnpore was as high as 120° in the shade. When we crossed into the United Provinces and eventually to the northern industrial city of Cawnpore, we found it was true. From here we marched the two miles to Wheeler Barracks, which was to be our home for the next three years.

These days one continually hears moans and groans about Britain's railway network. Anyone who had been with me on that crowded journey with no refreshments, with flies, intolerable temperatures and inadequate toilets, would find the trains of today super-travel.

B J HARRIS

INDIAN SUMMER

Denis Dowlan was a signaller with the 14th Field Regiment Royal Artillery in India.

The picture left shows Lord Louis Mountbatten taking the salute when the regiment were on parade in Karachi on August 14, 1947.

The picture below shows the 14th Field Regiment in action the following day.

GOD BLESS AMERICA

EVERY year, Thanksgiving brings back some vivid memories. On August 12, 1942, HMS Nigeria, the ship in which I served as a very ordinary seaman, was torpedoed in the Mediterranean. We had lost 48 ratings and marines and four officers.

With a huge patch to cover the hole in the ship's side, we sailed across the Atlantic to Charleston, South Carolina. From there, a party of us were sent by train to New York and an American naval base called Saker Two. Here my story really begins.

New York, New York, what a wonderful town! For men in uniform, almost everything was free - no matter which country you were from. In the stage door canteen, you rubbed shoulders with the stars and coffee and doughnuts were freely dispensed.

In the United Services building the Broadway shows were listed on a board. If a little yellow button showed, it meant free seats were available. I went to see Olsen and Johnson in Hellzapoppin'.

Another organisation gave free meals to servicemen and I dined with an American family and was written up in Colliers Weekly.

On Times Square, Coca Cola had a place where you paid a nickel for a hamburger, twenty pots of relish lined the counter and you could drink as much Coke as you wished for free. I was taken to a radio station to see Fred Wareing and His Pennsylvanians and to Radio City Music Hall to see a programme of films and the famous dance troupe The Rockettes.

I took the lift to the top of the Empire State building, 106 storeys high, and looked down on St Patrick's Cathedral.

I went to a charity bazaar where one only had to look at something to be asked: "You like that, sailor? It's yours".

Ron Stockwell - happy memories of US Thanksgiving

At Thanksgiving, the Navy boys ate well - as usual - with lashings of turkey. The following day, cold turkey was followed up with huge dollops of ice-cream.

Another warm memory was my romance with a Polish-American girl called Eleanor. I still carry her photograph in my wallet.

At last the day came when a party of us Brits were taken to the docks where the huge bulk of the Queen Mary loomed above us. There were four of us in cabin B120 and we made a successful passage to England.

RON STOCKWELL

SLIPPERY CUSTOMERS

A FRIEND and I, both in the RAMC as national servicemen in 1949/51, were doing our best to hitch-hike back to camp one night from just outside Yeovil, Somerset. It was about five miles, and although we weren't drunk, after a night on the tiles we were a bit unsteady on our feet so we were glad to see a lorry stop.

The two squaddies in the cab said: "Jump in the back, lads - we're going your way". We started off at top speed - the driver must have thought he was Mike Hawthorne.

It was pitch dark in the back of the lorry, which turned out to be the kind that was used to pick up engines and motor fittings.

The metal floor was covered in thick oil and grease - it was impossible to stand up on it without slipping and sliding about.

My mate and I spent most of the trip lying on our backs with our feet in the air. It was a nightmare - and to make matters worse, we could hear the driver and his mate laughing their socks off.

I was wearing my brand-new 'civvy' suit for only the second time - a smashing grey herringbone I'd saved up for months to buy.

When we did get back to camp, about half an hour later, I knew the pair had taken every country lane they could find, adding another five miles to the journey.

When we were dropped off, covered in axle grease and oil, we looked like an oil slick. We had to take baths in detergent before we could go to bed, and I could never wear that suit again.

Looking back now, I can see the funny side. I bet those drivers had a laugh about it for months afterwards. I just wish I could have met them when I was on MI room sick parade - I could have given them an injection and got my revenge!

MIKE DENNEY

Pte Mike Denney at Bovingdon Camp, Dorset

53

SPECIAL
OCCASIONS

VIP VISITORS

WE were Wrens working on the switchboard in Derby House in Liverpool. When Mr Churchill went to Canada to meet Mr Roosevelt in August, 1941, we connected a call from Liverpool to Newfoundland. That was exciting, although we knew we couldn't tell anyone.

Liverpool had lots of important visitors. Provided it wasn't secret, we were kept up to date with what was going on around us.

I did not see King George VI and Queen Elizabeth, but we all heard how the naval officers thought the Queen was wonderful and had the most beautiful complexion.

When we were told, at the last possible minute because of security, that Mrs Roosevelt was coming, it was arranged that the Wrens would be inspected.

We seldom drilled so we were not very good, but a dress rehearsal was arranged for the day before the visit. It was cold and damp but we marched behind a Marine band playing Hearts of Oak and halted on the pier head. All went well until the maintenance captain stopped in front of one young girl. He looked at her feet for a few seconds.

"Where did you get those shoes?" he asked. Although they were gleaming, it was certain they had not come from the naval clothing store.

"Lilley and Skinner, sir," was the unexpected reply.

Next day the Wrens, in dazzling white collars starched by the Chinese laundry and dazzling black shoes polished by themselves, fell in behind the marine

band. This time everything was perfect, or so everybody thought. Mrs Roosevelt stopped and exchanged a few words with one or two girls. The incident which caused most amusement was when she said to one Wren: "Your hat isn't the same as the others, is it?"

The Wrens had just changed from round-brimmed hats to the beret type. Everybody preferred the more jaunty image and the clothing store had none left. The Wren in question, using her initiative, had bought a beret and put an HMS hatband round it.

"No, ma'am," she admitted with a little embarrassment.

"Never mind," Mrs Roosevelt told her. "It's a very nice hat!"

The biggest bombshell of Mrs Roosevelt's visit was when she stayed the night at Ackerley House.

One solitary sailor, complete with rifle, stood outside guarding America's First Lady while inside the Wrens put on a show for their illustrious guest. She seemed to enjoy it - or maybe she was just being polite - and rose to thank them. She completely silenced them as she told them how much Admiral Sir Percy Noble would be welcomed in America.

I doubt if anyone but herself and the Admiral knew anything about this. Personnel movements of that kind were very hush-hush. To cross the Atlantic was an extremely risky business. However, Admiral Sir Percy Noble did just that in November 1942, and became Head of the British Admiralty delegation in Washington.

ISABEL ANDERSON

CORONATION DAY IN KOREA

DURING the early hours of June 2, 1953, before courtiers had begun to fuss over last-minute Coronation details, Easy-three, a dusty old 25-pounder I commanded in Korea, had engaged the enemy. While household regiments preened themselves resplendent in ceremonial dress, my gun crew and I had shared a communal shave in our smoke-blackened brew-can.

Even as workmen hung bunting along The Mall, we gunners of 107 Field Battery were hanging out our smalls to dry on lengths of knotted telephone wire.

At 1000 hours we joined the rest of our regiment, 20th Field RA, in firing a red, white and blue smoke-screen over enemy positions. In the afternoon, on the only piece of flat ground within the gun line, 107 Battery held a mini-gymkhana - greasy pole, three-legged race, sack race, egg and spoon race - and managed to forget the war for a couple of hours. Strangely, the enemy left us alone.

Three gun commanders were hard into the sack race when the CP gave out over the tannoy: 'TAKE POST'. It was hell trying to extract ourselves from those smelly rice sacks. Bombardier Dobson fell flat on his face, vowing to join the Navy. Bombardier Crossy and I collided and went straight into a 'come dancing' routine. The crowd loved it - and so did the wag who gave the bogus order.

The carnival mood lasted far into the evening as the Black Watch and the 61st Light Regiment RA fired an impressive Feu de Joie of red, white and blue flares high into the night sky. Then, from the hills of Yong-dong came a sound which stilled even the gods of war - a lone piper playing a salute to his Queen.

PETER STEPHENSON

OUR VE DAY 'ESCAPE'

I WAS a special wireless operator in the ATS, stationed near Harrogate.

On VE Day, the Harrogate local authority asked our CO to confine us to barracks, which seemed an extraordinary request after having served our country.

However, my friend and I escaped through a gap in the hedge and travelled by train to our homes in Middlesex. The Blue-Cap military police on duty at the camp must have spotted us, but shut their eyes!

JOYCE BOAST

THE DAY I CAPTURED A SPY

THREE of us had missed the morning PT. The main body of men would run up the road towards Greatstones, so we just hopped over the top and down the shingle of the Kent coast.

It was here I noticed something was wrong. The tide had gone out and left a small boat high and dry half-way up the sloping beach. I thought 'No fisherman would do that', so we went to investigate.

We found sacks of food, bottles of wine, and most surprising of all, an old radio.

This got us thinking, so we went back to camp to tell Captain Moore about our find. He stopped shaving, followed us back to the boat, and came to the conclusion that someone had landed in the night.

He gave to the order 'stand to' and we all lined up on the road. We hadn't gone very far before we spotted a man. He came out with his hands up, and I rushed forward to make sure he didn't play about with the other piece of his radio transmitter. He seemed to be enjoying the situation and said in perfect English: "I'll show you how it works".

At that, Captain Moore knocked the box out of his hands, saying: "You've played around with that long enough".

I collected all the German's belongings and took them with us. When we got back to the road Captain Moore interrogated him before we drove him off to Brigade HQ. On the way, he told us that he had set off from the French coast in a U-boat, towing his boat behind. He had got into it three miles from the English coast, paddling to the shore so as not to make a lot of noise.

I still wonder what would have happened if I hadn't caught that spy. Who knows - it might have changed the whole course of the war.

E OLIVER

L R Saunders is pictured (standing, right) among his army comrades in 1945

HOW I JOINED THE RWK REGIMENT

I well recall one small Tich Horn
Who looked at me and said with scorn,
"Your hair is long, you need a shave,
You'll be COFE and you'd best behave.
Here is your shilling, now draw your kit.
We'll do our best to make you fit."

I passed an officer called Major Lee
With a big red nose, who stared at me.
"He's your OC," said Corporal Mills.
"He's there to see you do your drills."
I had two jabs and a gas mask drill -
The test for gas made me feel quite ill.

The dentist said: "I'll just take two,
I'll stop three more and that should do."
I felt my arm begin to ache
But the barber said: "That's a piece of cake.
Wait until you've been here a week,
You'll feel whacked out
and have a job to speak."

"You're on fatigues," said Corporal Mills,
"And don't forget to take your pills."
The sick and lame were on parade
With arms hung limp (some looked afraid):
The cookhouse door was open wide,
The sergeant shouted "Come inside!

"You'll peel them spuds
and scrub the floor,
You'll not leave here until half past four."
We took our leave at five o'clock
With a mug of tea and a bun like rock.
The provost sergeant glared at me
And shouted out:
"I want a word with thee!

"To walk on square is mortal sin,
If I catch you again I'll run you in."
I felt like saying something rude
But walked away in a real foul mood.
L R SAUNDERS

THE TANK THAT SANK

THIS little incident happened in Normandy on June 9, 1944, three days after D-Day. We had all just had our 21st birthdays, having been afloat since mid-May, with 2nd Army HQ brass hats aboard.

We approached Juno Beach in daylight in our Liberty boat, with a Royal Navy crew, and attempted the first landing.

Down went the ramp - and the first tank rolled straight off into the briny and disappeared from view!

There was panic stations. Through a loud-hailer, the Canadian beachmaster yelled: "Nelson, take that bloody tug off and try again!"

Now all this time, I had positioned myself where I could keep my eyes on the spot where the tank disappeared - and I never saw it re-appear anywhere! (We succeeded in beaching at the first attempt, though.)

BARRIE HICKLING

PARADE GROUND GAFFE

AT an East Coast Bunting Tossers (Signallers Camp) during 1942, there was an acute shortage of buglers. To solve the problem, the top brass installed a Panatrope public address system, complete with a pile of records.

On the first day it went into operation, 500 men were assembled on the square. At one minute to nine, the signals bo'sun and the officer of the day were standing at the Panatrope base. The officer signalled at the bo'sun: 'Make it so, Bo'sun'.

From the loudspeaker, to a great roar of laughter, came the strains of "Clang, clang, clang went the trolley…". Some wag had put the wrong record on.

C A SHIERS

DRESSING FOR THE DANCE

IN the spring of 1945, I was with a detachment of ATS stationed on the East Coast. Our job was to help with the training of anti-aircraft batteries by photographing their gunfire in relation to the airborne target.

The monotony of being permanent staff at a location away from civilisation was relieved by having a garrison theatre where we were able to see the latest films and have a weekly dance to which outside units of the Army and RAF were invited.

Wearing uniform all the time soon began to pall and we asked if we could hold a Grand Dance and wear 'civvies'.

The camp commandant gave his permission, and with great joy, we kept the GPO on its toes by sending home for our dance frocks.

To our horror, three days before the big dance, a mixed battery arrived and we were told that it would be unfair to them if we wore our civilian clothes.

After much negotation, we were told we could make it a fancy dress dance.

Every minute of our spare time before The Day was filled with the preparation of white paper sashes such as beauty queens wore, on which we printed words picked out of the dictionary which started with 'mis' - Mis(S) Adventure to Mis(S) Use.

We wore the sashes over our frocks and we had a wonderful evening.

BETTY BAXTER

STARRY NIGHT OUT

IT was 1942 and as a WAAF, I was at an NCOs party held at Hook, in Surrey. The entertainment for the evening was a father/daughter act. The little girl, aged eight, was Petula Clark and we were all astounded by her talent. She and her father enacted a scene in which he was the master of the house who came into the kitchen to find the servant girl imitating Vera Lynn, Grace Moore and other stars, to perfection. Even at that young age, her performance was professional.

Later in the evening, her father asked me to partner him in a waltz competition and we won first prize. I was lucky that evening - I won two more boxes of chocolates as 'spot prizes' and gave one to Petula and her sister, who were sitting watching the dancing with their mother.

I bet Petula doesn't remember that evening as she was so young - but I do, and I'm 20 again whenever I think of it!

PHYL DOUGLAS

SHOW BIZ MEMORIES

HARRY Roy and his band entertained the troops when I was in Palestine in 1943. After the show, Harry came into the sergeants' mess, smiled and shook hands with us. Then, spotting our table tennis table, he asked if anyone would give him a game.

He had several games, playing all the table tennis fans in turn and not losing to a single one. I reckoned that if he hadn't been a band leader, he could have made his name in the table tennis world!

Years later, I was stationed at RAF Abingdon when I took my eldest son Michael and his friend to see Lonnie Donegan and his skiffle group, who were playing in Oxford.

After the show, both boys wanted to get the great man's autograph so we went round to the stage door. It was pouring with rain and we huddled in the doorway sheltering as best we could.

The doorman asked me to wait, and said that Mr Donegan would like to see the boys in his dressing room. They were there for some time, and returned, saying they had had a very pleasant chat with him.

My son still has his Lonnie Donegan records, and I have a memory of a very nice man who, despite his fame, found time to talk to two young fans.

ALF CARD

RACE AGAINST TIME

DURING the war, I was a driver for the Royal Navy and used to travel to dock-yards with goods for the ships and for Liverpool. One night in the middle of an air raid, we were on our way to one of the Royal docks when we came upon an ambulance.

The doors on each side at the front were open, and the engine was running but there was no sign of the driver or his partner. We decided to look inside. In the back was a lady in labour.

She said: "Please help - my baby's on the way". My mate John told me to take the ambulance while he went to the docks, so I started to drive. A policeman arrived on his motorbike. I gave him the details and he told me to follow him.

I have to say that was a thrilling ride. Me, a lad of 19, dashing across Liverpool, driving an ambulance with the bell ringing and escorted by two policemen on motorbikes. We arrived at a hospital and the lady was wheeled into a side ward.

The baby was born ten minutes later. I must admit I sat there crying my eyes out.

I was given a cup of tea and the nurse said I was in shock. After two hours of waiting, I was told the new mother would like to see me. I was taken into a small ward and greeted by the lady from the ambulance and her wonderful baby boy. She thanked me and asked me my name.

"Tom," I said.

"Well, my baby boy will be christened Tom."

A week later I returned to the hospital but mother and baby had gone home. We never met again. I never knew her name and all she knew of me was that I drove an RN van and my name was Tom.

TOM TUNSTALL

MEETING A STAR

WHILE I was doing my ATS training at Guildford in 1942, the film The Gentle Sex was being made, to help recruit more ATS girls.

When I was put in the same marching squad that the film's stars were in, I just couldn't believe it!

We were told not to bother Leslie Howard or any of the female stars for autographs. But when I left the factory where I worked before enlisting, the girls had given me an autograph book as a parting gift, so I was determined to get Leslie Howard's signature somehow.

I kept the book hidden away in my uniform pocket, and eventually 'collared' the star. When he asked if I knew we were not to bother him with requests for autographs, I said that yes, I did know, but that this was my first autograph book and his would be the first name in it. So he retired behind some vaulting horses to sign it without anyone else seeing.

GLADYS NEWLYN

Above: Gladys Newlyn persuaded Leslie Howard to sign her autograph book - against the rules

Right: Joyce McConnell's last photo in WAAF uniform before being demobbed in April, 1946

60

CONTRASTING CELEBRATIONS

ON May 8, 1945, I was stationed at a small maintenance unit at Barton Mills, near Mildenhall, Suffolk, when I was woken up at midnight by the sound of distant music and explosions.

We all sat up in bed and listened for a while. As soon as the noise stopped, we went back to sleep. Next morning we found out that the war in Europe had ended.

A month later, I was posted to a huge USAAF base at Burtonwood, near Warrington. One night, I was again woken up at midnight by music and a lot of noise. This time it seemed to be coming nearer and nearer.

We all hopped out of bed, put on uniform over our pyjamas, and set off together to find the source. Coming down the lane towards our compound was an American band, followed by what seemed like hundreds of GIs. Firecrackers were being thrown everywhere and there was great hilarity.

As they passed our gates, they came in and took our hands, and off we all went together, singing away to the music of Glenn Miller and Benny Goodman. We realised it was VJ Night, and the Americans' war was over, too.

Round the lanes we went, singing all the way. Finally the band stopped back at our gates and, with a roll of drums, a GI wearing a grass skirt and a garland leapt onto the roof of a nearby hut, and danced the hula-hula to a beautiful Hawaiian tune.

The crowd fell silent - it was an especially poignant moment at 2am in the middle of the Lancashire countryside.

As we filed back through the gates and the GIs disappeared down the lane, still playing their music, a van drove into the compound with a WAAF officer sitting on the bonnet, her cap all askew.

"Come on, everyone, who's for dancing the night away?" she yelled. The recreation hut was opened, a record player found, and we all stayed there for another hour or so. I think it was about 4am when we got back to bed.

What a contrast - the quiet acceptance of RAF Barton Mills on VE Night and the spontaneity of the USAAF base on VJ Night. I shall never forget it.

JOYCE McCONNELL

MY OLYMPIC APPEARANCE

WATCHING the Olympics on TV reminded me of the time I took part in a sports event in an Olympic stadium - the one at Athens where the first modern Olympic Games were held in 1896.

In 1945, when our battalion of the East Surrey Regiment was stationed in Greece, I was asked to pick and train a team for headquarters company to compete in the battalion sports meeting - just two weeks away. I got this job because I was the only PE instructor in the battalion.

I managed to train up a team and put myself down for three or four events and, to everyone's surprise, our team won the meeting.

After this success, I was asked to train a tug-of-war team to compete in a sports meeting of all the land forces in Greece.

I had some experience in tug-of-war as I had been a member of the team which won the Army championship in England in 1936.

We won our matches against all the other regiments in the brigade, and then against all the regiments in the division.

As divisional champions, we were at last booked to appear in the Land Forces Greece sports meeting held in June, 1945.

We were stationed up-country, but now the tug-of-war team went down to Athens for further training, billeted in a big house near the royal palace.

We would train all morning, keeping the afternoons free to go swimming before training again in the evening. We trained hard as we really wanted to win, keeping to a strict regime with no boozing and no late nights.

When it came to the big event, we felt privileged to be competing in the old Olympic stadium where so many world-class athletes had appeared.

A team from the Royal Artillery were considered to be the favourites in the tug-

of-war event and we were due to pull against them. Quite a number of our men had managed to attend so there was a good deal of betting going on.

The pull took place in the middle of the stadium. No other events were going on and all eyes were upon us.

We won the first pull and the Royal Artillery won the second, so the outcome centred on the third.

After a long struggle, we won that, too, and became the tug-of-war champions of Greece.

It was my one and only Olympic appearance.

C MONKS

The Pai-de-Hai Pin-ups of 1945 - Jack Jackson is second on the left

THE PIN-UP GIRLS

THE need for Ack-Ack regiments lessened by the end of 1942, and the following year I was posted overseas with the Royal Engineers to Paiforce (Persia and Iraq Force).

In the stifling heat of South Persia, live entertainment for the troops featuring well-known stars was rather thin on the ground, so some units formed their own concert parties.

Ours was called The Madhatters, and it produced three shows in just over two years.

The last was called Pai-de-Hai, and was staged at the area's Garrison Theatre in April, 1945.

One of the high spots was a spoof beauty contest called Pai Pin-Ups - a contest to find the most beautiful 'girl' in Paiforce.

I was listed as Koramshah Kate. The music was to come from the canteen piano, until some local lads decided to help out with guitars and drums.

Unknown to the cast some idiot, probably tanked up on the Canadian beer served in the canteen, coupled the obviously non-English names of the volunteer musicians with the spoof names of the pin-ups and started the rumour that the 'girls' were indeed girls and that the contest was for real!

On the first night, the show opened to a full house, and as the MC announced the beauty parade and the band struck up, the four 'ladies' in the photograph danced - not very gracefully - into view.

Boos, whistles and catcalls from disappointed customers nearly drowned out the music - but in true showbiz tradition, the show carried on!

JACK JACKSON

63

TIME FOR ROMANCE

FOR YOUR EARS ONLY

WHILE we were serving in Malaya in the late 1940s, one of my mates received a recorded disc from his girlfriend in England. He was at a loss as to how to play it so he asked me if I had any ideas. There was a radiogram in the orderly room and, as I knew one of the clerks, I asked him if he would play it for my mate.

We placed the record carefully on the turntable, my friend standing with his ear close to the speaker in order not to miss one word of the very intimate and loving message that followed.

After we had heard it twice, we switched off and returned to company lines.

Only then were we told that the message had been heard by the entire camp - the clerk had forgotten to turn off the loud-speakers!

S BATES

AN EXPENSIVE NIGHT OUT

IN 1939 my ship, HMS Effingham, was in Bermuda. My mate Ken and I had made friends with two girls in Hamilton, but there was one slight snag - money! Bermuda was very expensive and our pay was about a pound a week.

One evening Ken and I were going ashore to meet the girls at one of their houses but we only had six shillings each.

Ken suggested we should be exceptionally nice to the mother and tell her how wonderful it was to be able to sit in a house and feel really civilised again.

Our flattery worked. The girls seemed quite happy sitting indoors with us, and mother cooked us a wonderful meal. We played cards and board games and the time passed very quickly.

At 10pm we were thinking we'd had a great time without spending any money, so perhaps we could manage a stroll in the moonlight before saying goodnight and getting a bed in the seamen's hostel.

Our plan was scuppered when one of the girls suggested we go dancing. Ken and I said it was surely too late and looked to the mother for support. Alas - we had made too good an impression and she was only too happy for the girls to go with us.

They were keen to go to a new hotel, which meant taking a ferry to a nearby island.

I told Ken to go on ahead while I bought the tickets and was relieved that it had only cost two shillings for the four of us. If I could manage not to spend any more, I would have the fare back and two shillings left for our beds in the hostel. I quietly warned Ken to be careful as he would have to pay for everything else.

The hotel was obviously very expensive. I said I wasn't all that thirsty and I'd have a lemonade. Ken said he'd have one too. The girls ordered a John Collins each - we didn't know what a John Collins was but we guessed it would be dear. I saw my mate blanch when the waiter asked for six shillings.

The girls scarcely had time to sip those drinks. We were on the floor for every dance. We danced dances we had never heard of. Rumbas, sambas, bossa novas, tangos - you name it, we attempted it. The girls thought it was great fun, and by about 1am we were exhausted. Then came the cabaret. The girls finished off their drinks while we sipped ours exceptionally slowly.

At about 2.30am, we wended our weary way to the ferry. I asked for four tickets and put down two shillings. The ferryman said nothing, but pointed to a notice which, to my horror, said that fares were doubled after midnight. I used the rest of my money and caught up with the others.

We saw the girls home and then I had to tell Ken the sad news. There was no bed for us that night - we had to sleep on the beach.

ERIC WOOTTEN

JITTERBUG JITTERS

EVERYONE has certain tunes which remind them of particular episodes in their lives. I only have to hear Glenn Miller's In The Mood for my mind to skip back to the days when I was introduced to the jitterbug.

At 18, I had joined the RAF seeking excitement, travel and adventure. The war had ended two years previously and I found myself at RAF Wythall dishing out clothing coupons, ration cards and travel warrants to veterans being demobbed.

At RAF Wythall - or as we wittily dubbed it RAF Without - some six miles from Birmingham, I hadn't even seen an aeroplane.

There was some novelty in sharing a tin hut with 29 other girls, and sleeping head to tail on iron beds, but this quickly palled.

For entertainment there was ping-pong and pool, and a cinema where the film usually broke down in the middle. And then there were the Friday night informal dances in the NAAFI.

I'd made friends with a tall blonde girl from Glasgow named Irene, and for lack of anywhere else to go, we went to the dances most Fridays. One night there was a group of American airmen leaning languidly on the bar. We wondered who'd invited them - they didn't seem interested in dancing.

We soon forgot them as we paired off for a slow foxtrot followed by a waltz. The airman in charge of the music then put on In The Mood.

The Americans were suddenly galvanized into life. Within seconds they'd claimed partners and were frenziedly spinning them and flinging them aloft with nonchalant assurance.

I was astounded. This was serious stuff. To my alarm, I saw a tall, dark type approaching me with a purposeful look in his eye.

"Would you like to dance, ma'am?" he asked, his smile revealing perfect teeth.

"I'm sorry," I said. "I can't do this, I'd just embarrass you."

"Aw, c'mon," he said. "It's a breeze. Just jump when I say jump."

I was whisked on to the floor, whirled around dizzily, swung from left hip to right hip, up over his head, down through his legs and back on my feet again.

"Hey, you're doing fine," he said, spinning me around again. "Jump!" His hands round my waist, he swung me up higher than ever, and down again I swooped. I slipped through his legs, and he let go.

I continued on, suspenders flashing, skittering across the floor like a rocket as the other grinning dancers parted like the Red Sea. Eventually I came to a halt, covered in confusion and chalk dust.

My partner was full of apologies. "Gee, I'm sorry, ma'am," he said. "I somehow lost my balance and loosed my grip. Are you OK?"

"No bones broken," I replied, "but I think I'll sit this one out."

A cheer broke out from a few grinning airmen nearby as he helped me to my feet. I walked with what dignity I could muster to a nearby table.

My partner followed me, still apologising. He told me his name was Reno dal Rosa and he came from Pennsylvania. I looked at him doubtfully. Nobody has a name like Reno dal Rosa. It sounded like an Italian holiday resort.

"My folks came from Italy," he explained. He spoke of the family back home that he hadn't seen for two years, and how he hoped to go back to medical school when he'd left the Air Corps.

The Yanks had acquired a somewhat dubious reputation since their arrival. Explicit invitations to them to return whence they came had been daubed on many a blank wall. But this was a courteous young man who seemed to be an all-round 'good egg', despite his having

A FACE FROM THE PAST

THROUGH a bizarre chain of events, quite out of the blue, I was given the address and phone number of a girl I used to work with during the war.

Jeanne and I met when we were posted to an intelligence unit at fighter command HQ - no ordinary posting, but a trip to heaven, for we'd been seconded to the American Air Corps.

To the much-travelled youngsters of today it would be hard to describe the thrill of hearing 'real' American voices for the first time and to work alongside tall men in olive green battle-dress who really did chew gum and smoke cigars.

But it was the luxury of our new environment that impressed us. Accustomed to wartime austerity, we found ourselves eating steaks, cream, fresh fruit - the kind of food we hadn't seen for years. We were able to shop in the PX (the Post Exchange - the American equivalent of our NAAFI), an Aladdin's cave of Chesterfield cigarettes, canned fruit juice and Hershey Bars.

Jeanne and I were responsible for drawing graphs and charts showing battle statistics to be used for the invasion.

We had special passes that took us into the ops room with its large table-top map on which units of the WAAF plotted air activity over the Channel. It was here that we saw the first flying bomb on its way across the South of England.

It disappeared from the map right over my home and I spent several days praying that my family were unharmed - they had already been bombed out of our house in London.

Total security prevented me from contacting them, but fortunately, a letter from my mother showed that everything was

Patricia Vinton was persuaded to try the jitterbug by a tall, dark GI

hurled me to the floor so carelessly.

After the dance, I never saw him again. But whenever I hear In The Mood, I'm 18 again and back with the man with the improbable name who tried to teach me to jitterbug.

PATRICIA VINTON

OK. Jeanne and I celebrated with Coke, a strange fizzy concoction that was nowhere near as good as Tizer.

Life was idyllic and we spent sunny evenings sitting on the grass listening to the station band - a rare privilege, because the band was the Glenn Miller Orchestra!

But overshadowing everything else was the fact that I shared a small office with the most beautiful girl on the post.

We chatted, we shopped together and we exchanged confidences. I adored her.

Alas, there was no fairy tale ending. She married a high-ranking RAF officer and I was sent to France to work with General Eisenhower.

I am ashamed to admit that in the intervening years I had forgotten her - 50 years is a long time. But how shattered I was when I discovered she had kept a photograph of me - and one of my letters!

BERNARD WILKIE

STRANGERS
ON A TRAIN

ONE hot May night after the war in Europe was over, I was going home and had taken off my cap and tie. Just as the train was pulling out of Waterloo, an RAF officer jumped into the carriage.

Horrors! Did the RAF have jurisdiction over a mere ATS private I wondered. I needn't have worried - by the time the train reached Wimbledon we had made a date at Hampton Court for next day.

He met my mother, I met his parents - and six weeks after our first encounter, we were married. Everyone said it wouldn't last, but we celebrated our golden wedding in 1995. Sadly, my beloved died - but I'm sure we shall meet up again in another life.

BETTY ROEBUCK

WEDDING BELLS

This wedding group from 1944 was sent in by Dorothy Pine. The bride, she says, wore 'borrowed plumes' and the flowers came from the vicar's garden.
Friends and family still managed to arrange a reception, with a three-tier wedding cake - which had been iced using powdered milk!

STARTING OUT

WINIFRED Hutton and her husband Frederick were both in uniform when they married on May 23, 1942, at St Henry and St Elizabeth RC Church in Sheerness, Kent.

He was a chief petty officer in the Royal Navy and Winifred was a WAAF.

CPO Hutton was three times involved in the Russian convoy operations, and his wife's WAAF service included a spell on balloons in London.

PROPOSAL OVER THE AIRWAVES

I MET my wife Irene during the war. We were both entertainers, rehearsing for a show called Stars in Battledress.

I liked her from the start because, after a rehearsal, we went out for a meal and she insisted she pay for her own - my Army pay wasn't enough.

We toured all the South Coast, did 20,000 miles around Germany and were always together. When we came back to England, we got engaged.

Then I was demobbed, and went on the stage as a comedian. Irene was promoted to sergeant and sent out to Germany in charge of a hostel for army entertainers.

A few months later, I was doing a broadcast with Delroy Summers and his band. My act on this show was as a nervous soldier who had never been on the stage before.

So I asked the producer if I could propose to my fiancee over the wireless. He said I could only do it in comedy. So I had a violin playing Hearts and Flowers near the microphone, and here's what I said:

"My little flower of the Persian Desert, my Mam says if you could get home for the 21st of December, she will let you marry me."

When my fiancee heard the broadcast, she told her officer and they gave her a party. They flew her home the next day and we were married the day after that.

We have never been separated since. We were a double act on the stage, going by the name of Maurice Burns and Irene.

I am 81 now and Irene is 72. We have two children. Our boy is an entertainer in New Mexico, and our daughter is a music teacher.

MAURICE HALL

LUCKY NUMBER 13

THE number 13 plays a large part in my story. When I was called up into the RAF, I lived in a house with No 13 on the door.

I carried this number in my wallet throughout the war and when I was posted to West Africa in 1943, the date was December 13.

The convoy I sailed in was attacked in the Atlantic by 13 U-boats.

Just after VE Day, while I was stationed in Scotland, I was posted back to England to an airfield just outside Worcester - on the 13th day of the month.

The first airman I met turned out to come from Liverpool, and we became friends.

One weekend we were given a 48-hour weekend pass, and my mate asked if I would like to go back to Liverpool and meet his wife and children.

We cycled the nine miles into Worcester and then hitch-hiked to Liverpool. When we arrived at the house, another young lady was there, too.

She was my mate's wife's sister, and I knew as soon as I was introduced to her that she was the person I wanted to share the rest of my life with. It seemed as though we had always known each other.

Her name was Pearl - and she was a gem. Pearl and I were married when I left the RAF.

We had 40 wonderful years together, four children and six grandchildren.

JACK THOMSON

A LOST LOVE FOUND

IN 1943, I joined the WAAF and trained as a nurse. The following year I became engaged to an Australian pilot. We were very much in love.

On a day out in London, we went on a guided tour of the Houses of Parliament. Frank, my Aussie sweetheart, sat me down in the Speaker's Chair and asked me to marry him.

When I answered 'yes', he put a lovely diamond and sapphire ring on my engagement finger.

At the end of the war, Frank was repatriated to Australia, and I was posted to Hamburg.

We arranged that I would eventually go to Australia and marry him, but when the time came, I got cold feet and couldn't leave my parents. Australia seemed so far away in those days.

I returned his ring, and never heard from him again.

In 1985, after a 40-year career in nursing, I went to Australia to visit friends, and while I was there, began to wonder whether my Aussie pilot was still alive and what sort of life he had had.

I went to his old home in Brisbane, but could find no-one who knew him. He had been a staunch Catholic, so a friend approached the local Catholic church for me, and found that his brother was still a regular worshipper there.

Through him, Frank phoned me and asked me round to meet his wife and family.

When the car drew up outside his house, all I could see was a good-looking dark curly-haired pilot - but in reality Frank was now a grey-haired elderly gentleman, waiting for me in his garden.

We hugged each other and all those 40 years fell away. I found out that life had been good to Frank - he had eight children, all of whom were doing very well.

EDITH ADCOCK

Above: Edith Adcock, better known as Bobbie Gibbs during her WAAF service

HOSPITAL GIFTS

Helen Collett, pictured in her Land Army uniform, remembers some 'loyal friendships' during her wartime service.

"At one point, I was admitted to hospital with appendicitis, and at least four of the girls would come at visit me each evening," she recalls.

"They used to bring me a few sweets from their rations, and on one occasion, they managed to bring an egg for my breakfast - with my name written on it, as eggs were rationed!"

MEETING RITA

I GOT my wartime call-up papers when I was just 18, going into communications at West Prawle, Devon, with the Royal Artillery.

We had an outside line to the RAF switchboard and after a time, I got chatting to the WAAF operator.

I began to look forward to the times she was on duty. She would pass our hut on her way up to the operations block. My friend George used to go out and speak to her but I was too naive and reserved to do the same. I just watched her from the window. She looked so lovely - even in uniform.

One day when we were chatting on the phone, my sergeant cut in and told us: "It's about time you two got out to meet each other and stopped wasting the batteries!"

He broke the ice for me - and changed my life. In the next year Rita and I got to know each other, went out together, and met each other's parents.

Then I was posted to the Royal Army Service Corps, taught to drive and sent to the ambulance car company, going out to France on D-Day 4.

I wrote to Rita and asked her to become engaged to me. She accepted and we managed to get leave together a couple of times.

We eventually married in 1947 - and it doesn't seem like 55 years since we first met.

DENNIS EVANS

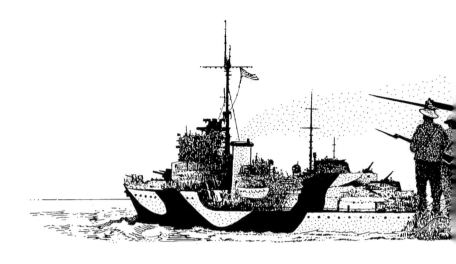

WAS MY FACE RED!

CALLING TO THE COWS

AS a member of the Women's Land Army, at Sparsholt Training Farm in 1942, we were up at 5am, and allowed a cup of cold milk before milking. We were taught how to machine-milk and hand-milk cows.

Most of the milking was under cover in the cowshed, but I had to hand-milk one cow out in an open pen and it was very cold and frosty. We had to clean the cowshed out with some of the largest and heaviest buckets and brooms I have ever used.

When it was my turn to fetch the cows down from the field in the dark early one morning, I could just see one right at the top of the hill which would not come to

my call, so I went up to find out what was wrong. I felt so stupid - I'd been calling to a bush!

I never lived that down all the time I was at Sparsholt.

Coming from London, I had never had anything to do with hurricane lamps. One morning, while working on a farm near Banbury, I went into the cowshed and saw the farmer had left one alight, there was no electricity, of course. Thinking of saving paraffin, I turned the wick down until it went out.

The air was blue the next morning when I went into work - the farmer had spent nearly half an hour trying to get the wick back up with a safety pin at 5am in the dark cowshed. It was his only means of lighting. I was not very popular for a few days.

JOAN CLIFFORD

NOTHING TO WEAR

I SIGNED up for 10 years service in the RAF at Padgate on June 27, 1946. We sat in draughty rooms for over 10 days awaiting pay books, 1250s and various aptitude tests. The days were endless. Our civilian clothes got dirtier and dirtier.

All documentation completed, we were sworn in as loyal subjects of His Majesty.

The food was totally uneatable. We seemed to queue for hours. We were so homesick for our mothers' cooking. But being young, ignorant and stupid, we thought we could cope with anything. And we did.

At last the big day arrived, and we were marched to the huge clothing store. The next two hours were like something from Monty Python or the Goon Show.

I was only 5ft 3in tall then and very slight in build. I weighed about eight stone - not exactly a common service shape.

The clothing store WO took one look at me and laughed out loud. "How the hell are we going to fit out this freak?" he exclaimed to one of the equipment assistant sergeants.

I was left practically until last. Nothing fitted - uniforms, boots, socks, shoes or underwear. As for my webbing equipment, it was a joke. It never fitted properly - even 10 years later. Finally, in desperation, the station tailor was sent for. Could he make me look reasonably airman-like? He measured me and chalked me. I looked like a snowman by the time he had finished.

I was told to wait two days for all the alterations to my uniforms. My trousers looked like bell-bottoms. I had more deficiency chits for kit and clothing than anyone in my flight.

My humiliation was completed by my new flight lieutenant. "How do they expect the RAF to kit out a short-arsed Welshman?", I heard him say to the Sgt DI.

I was only 17 years and 10 months old, and had never left home before. What an introduction to what was to be my next 10 years. Thank God I had a sense of humour.

By the way, one item of clothing did fit - my cap. I had the largest head in the flight.

CLIFFORD THOMAS

HAVEN'T I HEARD THIS BEFORE?

IN 1942, I was a member of an ATS guard of honour in Shrewsbury for the then Princess Royal. She stopped near me and asked me: "Do you enjoy service life?" "Very much, Ma'am," I replied.

Four years later, in 1946, I was again in a guard of honour, this time in a victory parade, when the Princess Royal visited our training camp in London.

She stopped near me and asked me: "Do you enjoy service life?" To my horror, I heard myself replying: "You have already asked me that". After a silence which seemed to last forever, the Princess moved on. The look on the face of the officer who was accompanying her will stay with me forever.

JOAN GETLIFFE

Right: Joan as an ATS corporal in 1944

NAMED - AND SHAMED!

DURING my three-week basic training in Scotland for the ATS in April 1941, my friend and I decided to visit Edinburgh on our day off. Off we went in our smart new uniforms. Walking proudly along Princes Street, we were abruptly stopped by two military policemen.

"Aye, aye," said one, "what have we here? Scott and Russell!" How did they know our names, we wondered. Then we realised we had worked the names on the wrong side of our gas mask straps - and everyone could see who we were!

CHRIS SKINNER

GETTING THE BIRD

DURING my National Service days in Germany, I was once reprimanded by our platoon sergeant for scattering pieces of bread on the grass for the birds.

Some days later while attending a muster parade, a low-flying pigeon dropped a large deposit, which scored a direct hit on my face as I stood to attention.

The inspecting sergeant, who'd earlier rebuked me, saw it happen and with a large grin on his face, remarked: "That'll teach you to feed those damned pigeons".

ALAN PETLEY

GETTING DOWN
TO BASICS

I FOUND that life in the Women's Land Army was quite an education after working in an office in Liverpool.

My boss was termed a 'gentleman farmer', which meant he didn't get his hands dirty, while our jobs were down to basics - the most basic involving cleaning out the cattle and pig pens.

When we arrived at work each day at 8am, one of us would report at the house for our orders, while the other would store our bikes away and get the tools needed for the day.

One one occasion, I knocked at the door to ask, though I had a good idea of what that day's job would be.

"Good morning," said my boss. "I think we'll have you both on the manure spreading."

"It's muck spreading!" I shouted back to my mate as she approached the tool shed.

"Not b——- s—- slinging again!" she complained.

Aghast, I turned round to look at the boss's face - but he had scarpered, doubtless unnerved by such language.

THELMA PENNELL

RUDE AWAKENING

MY pals and I were in Germany in 1944. Shells were falling all around us as the orders came to vacate the lorries in which we were sleeping.

We already had our clothes on, so we hurriedly put on our boots, jumped out, and ran towards the hedge. Suddenly we heard someone yell: "I've been hit, I've been hit!"

Crowding around him, we struck a match and found the cause of the casualty's trouble - he'd got his boots on the wrong feet!

IVAN POPE

RED FACE
IN THE BAND

REMEMBER how, during the war, children had to make their own entertainment? We had trips to the swimming baths, Saturday cinema, and Sunday morning Boys' Brigade bands.

I was a very proud solo drummer in a band led by 17-year-old Terry. When Terry got his call-up papers, the bandmaster asked me if I would take over as drum-major. Would I! I had been spending every spare minute practising twirling, throwing - and sometimes even - catching. If Gran called on us, she didn't dare put her walking stick down.

I was a very young-looking 16-year-old and in a feeble attempt to speed up the ageing process, I attempted to grow a moustache. Being fair-haired, the result was more Betty Grable than Clark Gable. In a feeble attempt to redress the problem, I used a light application of soot. This seemed to work reasonably well, but also inherited me the nickname of 'Tasher' from my workmates, including Mr Lowery, who had an enormous capacity for liquid refreshment.

I was proud of my new position of drum-major. The British Legion asked our band to front them at the Armistice Day parade and service. We were to assemble and march through the streets. I was really looking forward to doing my stuff - until it occurred to me that the parade route was on Mr Lowery's patch and involved passing his favourite pub. Still, I thought, the chance of him seeing me was pretty remote.

We assembled, watched by a hundred or so spectators. As leader, and because I had no one to follow, my directional instructions came from the bandmaster with blasts on a whistle - one for a right turn and two for a left.

I would raise the four-foot silver and chrome mace aloft and, depending on the number of whistles, swing it to indicate which direction the parade was to take.

I was a little nervous, and as we approached the pub, as luck would have it, Mr Lowery came out with glass in hand.

This so unnerved me that on hearing the whistle I signalled a very uncertain right turn without waiting for a second blast. I took the right turn alone as the drummers and the parade went left.

I wished the ground would open up and and swallow me. To compound my embarrassment, I heard Mr Lowery's voice boom out: "Hey, Tasher, they've gone down t'other bloody way!"

DENNIS THORNTON

FLAMING HECK!

IN 1942, I was a 17-year-old WAAF driver on duty in the fire section at RAF Padgate. I drove the fire engine - a boring job since we never had any fires.

One day as the crew were sitting around playing cards, I took the fire tender down to the MT section to fill up with petrol. I was filling up from cans when the MT corporal-in-charge suddenly shouted: "Fire in 3 Wing!"

"Something exciting at last!" I thought. I got into the fire tender and sped over there, arriving to cheers from the RAF recruits.

Then I realised I'd forgotten to bring the fire crew with me!

As I sped back to the main camp, I met them coming down to 3 Wing on their bikes, all pedalling furiously.

The wrath - delivered in some words I'd never heard before - of the flight sergeant as they climbed aboard the fire tender, I shall never forget.

WINNIE TUNSTALL

Left: Winnie Tunstall, then Winnie O'Mara, in uniform

YES, SIR, IT'S ME!

IN 1943 I was attached to a French air force flight to assist with the language problems. Following an accident on the airfield, I took charge of an inquiry and while I was marching various witnesses in to the investigating officer, a corporal PTI/policeman called me by name - Harris!

I found myself facing my old French teacher.

W OWEN HARRIS

A LEAP
TO DISASTER

AS a Land Girl, I was standing on top of the thresher when a mouse jumped out of a corn sheaf in mid-air and fell straight down the back of my open-necked shirt.

Fortunately I had a belt round my waist, so the mouse was confined to the top half of me. It was running round and round inside my shirt, and I was screaming blue murder.

Relief, of sorts, was at hand. Seeing what had happened, a farmhand bounded up the ladder to me, grabbed a handful of shirt with the mouse inside it, and held onto the fabric until the creature was dead.

After that, I always buttoned my shirts up to the neck and tied pieces of string round the bottom of my trouser legs.

SYLVIA HARPER

Right: Isobel in 1945

SHARING A SLEEPER

I WAS stationed with the Royal Signals in Ghent, Belgium, in June 1945, and my Canadian cousin Tom Stewart was stationed in Paris. We both spent our leave with my parents in Aberdeen.

When it was over, I was to return to Ghent the night before Tom went back to Paris, so Tom volunteered to book us both sleepers on our respective trains for the 12-hour overnight trip down to London.

All the family came to see me off. I handed my sleeper ticket to the guard. He looked at me and asked: "Who's travelling?"

I turned out to have been booked into a sleeping compartment with three fellows - two RAF officers and a harbour master porter!

The train was full, so I couldn't be transferred.

Nowadays no-one would bat an eyelid, but back in 1945 the sleeper attendant was most concerned and spent the night opening the door occasionally to make sure I was all right. A timid 20-year-old, I was snuggled up in the bottom bunk.

I think he stopped all four of us from sleeping soundly - and my three travelling companions all turned out to be gentlemen.

ISOBEL CAULTON

HOME COMFORTS

TREAT THAT WENT WRONG

IN the winter of 1942, I was a supply Petty Officer in the Royal Navy, and my fellow Petty Officer was Fred Bee. On our way by train to Greenock in Scotland, we found that we had a lot in common. We were both to go into lodgings at Greenock with a Mrs MacTaggart.

On our arrival, Mrs MacTaggart's door swung open to reveal a tall, stern-looking lady, who lost no time in laying down the rules of the house.

They were pretty stringent but quite fair, and we soon found that she also had a soft side - as long as we kept to her rules. In fact, she was like a mother to us at times.

We were with her about six weeks, until we received a letter ordering us report to Troon.

I think it was Fred who suggested that it would be a nice gesture to buy our landlady a present in appreciation of her kindness. What could we get her? She wasn't the type to accept a bunch of flowers, and we couldn't think of anything else.

Fred had the solution. What about taking Mrs Mac out to the cinema, with a nice fish and chip supper afterwards?

We approached her with our proposal. At first she went quiet, and gave us a look of distrust - I'm sure she thought we were pulling her leg. But she relented, and we made arrangements to leave about six o'clock.

At ten minutes to six, we walked to the bus stop, Fred and I on either arm of Mrs Mac, who was all dolled up in her Sunday

best. There were about five people in the bus queue. When the bus came along, we gallantly helped Mrs Mac onto the platform, and made to follow her - but the conductor put his hand on my chest and said: "Sorry, chum, we're full up". And away went the bus, leaving us standing flabbergasted on the pavement.

It was a long time before we could board another bus, and even longer to find the cinema that Mrs Mac had decided on, as we had kept this side of the event a surprise.

But eventually we found her standing in the foyer of one. Her face was red with rage, and she was tapping her foot in a most disturbing way. We tried to tell her what had happened but all she said was: "Take me home". I am sure she never forgave us for it.

I would like to think that Mrs Mac did at last forgive us, and realise our intentions were sincere.

Fred won't be reading this, for both our brand-new ships went mine-sweeping in the North Sea about three weeks after leaving Mrs Mac's. Fred's ship hit a mine, and was blown to smithereens. I was privileged to know him for the short and happy time that I did.

R W RUFFE

SANTA IN THE SNOW

ONE Christmas when I was in married quarters in Warminster, the snow-covered street made such a lovely scene.

The Salvation Army band came to play under a street lamp. It was followed by a lorry covered in Christmas tree branches and decorations, with Santa Claus sitting in the middle playing carols on a record-player.

There was a knock at my door and I opened it to find a man collecting for the town's old people. He saw my two small daughters, aged three and five, and called to Santa, who by this time was at the end of the street.

Santa got down off the lorry and walked up the street to my two little girls to shake hands and talk to them.

I shall never forget the look on their faces or the sight of Santa walking through the snow. When he had gone, they dashed up to their bedroom to see him leave on the lorry, waving to them.

Those two little girls now have children of their own and I love telling them about the time Santa Claus came walking through the snow to see their mums.

IRENE ROBINSON

A FULL ENGLISH BREAKFAST

I WAS called up for Army service on August 15, 1940, at the age of 20. There were several young men with me on the train from London bound for Westward Ho in Devon, and when we arrived, we were walked - not marched - by our sergeant to a holiday camp.

"This can't be too bad," I thought - but, of course, it was just wishful thinking. We arrived at the holiday camp and were checked, with three men allocated to a chalet. We were not given anything to eat but were told we could go to the NAAFI.

In the morning, feeling hungry and still wearing our civvies, we assembled in the camp dining room. We were each issued with a tin bowl, tin plate, knife, fork and spoon.

We lined up and were first given a ladleful of runny porridge - on top of this was placed a kipper and a dab of jam - then two slices of bread and margarine. To finish off, the bowls were half-filled with tea.

We found seats and began our breakfast of a mixture of porridge, kipper, jam, and bread and marg. This must be the best "full English breakfast" I have ever 'enjoyed'.

MAURICE ILOTT

'CAPTURED' BY A LONELY COUPLE

THE first Christmas Day I spent as a member of the ATS was quite a mild day. I was stationed near Reading and after dinner, three of us went for a walk which took us into a wood where we sat on a log. After a few minutes, a very stern-looking gentleman came along and told us we were trespassing. He ordered us to follow him.

We were all worried and very apologetic, thinking we were going to be reported to our CO. We arrived at a large house where we were met by a sad-looking lady.

The gentleman told us that they had seen us out walking, and felt very lonely as they had recently lost their only son. We were invited to stay for tea before being escorted back to camp with an invitation to visit whenever we liked.

I kept in touch with this couple every year until their deaths, and after all these years I still fondly remember the Christmas I was 'captured' by a lonely couple.

ANN FARRANT

SMILING THROUGH

Mrs Joyce Partington, nee Hardman, vividly remembers the get-togethers her mother Elsie would put on for wounded soldiers at the family home at Sale, Cheshire.

"There was good food, and someone would always play the piano for a sing-song," she says.

"The local butcher could usually find us the odd pound of sausages, and when the soldiers saw them, they would burst into song with : 'Ah, sweet mystery of life....'

"They were always full of laughter and good humour, even though they had all been seriously injured."

Joyce is the girl in the centre of both photographs, taken at one of the get-togethers, standing next to the local vicar, Rev Snell. Her mother Elsie is next to him, with her friends and helpers Olive Jones, Bertha Owen and Elsie Beardsall.

THE POWER OF FLOWERS

WHEN my ship returned from duty in Singapore and the Far East in July 1942, the Royal Navy gave me shore duty for a while as a travelling escort. I was sent to collect sailors who had overstayed their leave and bring them back to naval barracks.

Now in my 80s, and a gardener, when I see chrysanthemums I often think of one young lad I had to collect from Ripley, in Yorkshire.

Like lots of youngsters, he had been called up for hostilities only, and was told to report just a month or so before the town's annual flower show. Up till then, he had devoted every spare minute to getting his prize chrysanthemums ready for display.

All the same, he responded to the call-up and after a few weeks in the navy, he was eligible for a long weekend's leave. He was due back to barracks by 8am on the Monday morning, but by the Friday of that week there was still no sign of him, and eventually I was sent to collect him from his local police station.

With two other escorts, I arrived by train at Ripley around midnight, where we were given accommodation at a special constable's home. The Special knew the lad well and told us what had happened.

It appeared that Albert, as the boy was called, was so obsessed with his flowers that he just had to stay and see them in the show. He won a couple of prizes, too.

We collected Albert from the police station. He was only a little lad, five feet nothing, but he knew all about chrysanths. (So did I by the end of the job.)

He asked if we could call in at his home on the way back, just to say goodbye to his mum. So we did, and he showed us all the cups and trophies he had won for growing chrysanths, along with some of his plants - more beautiful ones I have still to see.

Over the years I have tried to grow chrysanthemums myself, trying to remember Albert's tips - but I've never won any prizes for it!

REG T WILSON

'CIAO' TO ALL THAT

Ernie Smith (pictured below, on the left) well recalls the night he and his pal Steve Holder saw the sights of Rome when they were on leave at a rest camp there in 1945.

After a visit to the Forum, where the picture was taken, they made for a cafe to sample the local wine.

It wasn't until they got up to leave that they realised how strong it was. They didn't make it back to camp before curfew, and ended up sleeping 'on huge blocks of stone' in the Coliseum.

Next morning, they had a wash in one of Rome's fountains and a shave at a local barber's.

"Forty years later, I went back to Rome with my family to show them those blocks but they'd all been cleared away," says Ernie ruefully.

He and Steve are pictured again, above, in the garden of an Italian friend, Boris Bastida and his wife. Ernie is holding the couple's small son, Ezio.

The picture at bottom right shows Ernie with his regimental sergeant major outside the stores when he was stationed with the Royal Engineers at Warmbad, Austria, in 1946.

A RUM DO!

"UP Spirits!" During the times when ratings serving in the Royal Navy were issued with a daily ration of rum, the shrilling of the Quartermaster's daily 11.30am pipe was second in popularity only to the command of "Libertymen Fall In!"

The custom was only abandoned in the mid-1960s when a more liberal regime gave the lower-deck access to other forms of alcohol.

Naval service during World War II gave me an insight into this mystique. On joining a ship or shore establishment, each rating was given what was known as a Station Card which included one of three categories of rum entitlement. 'G' (Grog) indicated that the rating was entitled to draw a daily ration of rum and had elected to do so. 'T' (Temperance) meant that the individual wished to abstain and was paid threepence a day in lieu of rum. 'UA' (Under Age) applied to ratings under 18, who were too young to drink.

The term 'grog' appears to have originated in the 18th century when a certain Admiral Vernon ordered that naval rum be diluted with water to reduce drunkenness. As he habitually wore a cloak made of grogram, a coarse mixture of silk, wool and

A FULL LOAD

Stella Hookham of Huntingdon sent in this picture of Land Army girls and regular farm workers, taken in the summer of 1944 or 1945, at Cringle Farm, Wollaston, near Wellingborough.

mohair, the matelots suffering rum dilution likened the roughness of the cloth to the kind of justice they had received, and the admiral became known as Old Grog.

Aboard capital ships and shore bases, this dilution persisted until the end of the rum issue. On smaller craft, such as destroyers, corvettes and minesweepers, the captain would often permit the rum ration to be issued neat to help compensate for the discomfort of serving in these ships and to boost morale.

A Rum Bosun was elected by members of each mess, whose job was to draw the total quantity of rum due to his messmates from the point of issue and to meticu-lously measure out one tot (about one eighth of a pint) to all the 'G' category men.

He had to be trustworthy as any short-fall in tot levels was quickly detected and he was expected to make it good from his own ration.

Rum was used as a form of lower-deck currency. There had to be a scale of values. Four sips equalled one gulp and two gulps equalled one tot. These quantities were commonly known as 'sippers' and 'gulpers' respectively.

Messmates would offer each other a 'sipper' on such occasions as their birthdays or for any small favour such as swapping duties. 'Gulpers' were only parted with for some major event - a marriage, the birth of a child, or comparable occasions.

In the days of sail, the mainbrace was both the largest and the most difficult to splice, being placed in a lofty and highly dangerous position. When the hands had finished the perilous job, they received a double tot of rum.

Although this task had long since disappeared, its spirit and tradition lasted until the latter days of the rum issue. On memorable days such as the successful conclusion of an action and at the end of the war, the captain would order "Up Spirits" to be superseded by "Splice the Mainbrace!" - a phrase which has passed into English nautical history.

REG NEWTON

IN MEMORY OF A SECOND WORLD WAR SOLDIER

I loved my Uncle Herbert,
He showed me how to fall,
He was a parachutist,
He had a gun an' all.

He jumped off t'air raid shelter
And landed on our lawn.
I jumped out of the window
And all my leg got torn.

My Mam was mad with Herbert,
"Get off home", she said,
"Showing off to kiddies,
You must be wrong in t'head."

When we heard that he'd been killed,
My Mam she took it bad,
I loved my Uncle Herbert
But I'm glad it wasn't Dad.

FRANCES BROOK

RECITAL FOR ONE

AS the Allied armies advanced into Europe during the winter of 1944, I was billeted with a Belgian family. One of the adults recognised a tune I was whistling as coming from a Hollywood film, and remarked that his daughter was studying to become a concert pianist.

He told me he would get her to give me a full piano version of the work - the tune had been taken from Chopin's Fantaisie-Impromptu.

The recital was given by the young pianist on the instrument she practised on at home, to possibly the smallest audience she would ever have. She played well, though I have never heard of her since.

A peep into the family's pantry revealed tins of American-produced food, which suggested that a member of the American forces was a welcome visitor. Perhaps the young musician eventually settled in the USA.

E W CHANNELL

Right: E W Channell - a private piano recital

THE OLD KIT BAG

THE first kit bags we were issued with in the WAAF during the war were the same as the men's. Later, a sausage-shaped one with handles was introduced which was easier to carry with all our kit in it. I still have mine, though it is faded now.

It was, and still is, useful - I took it on many caravan holidays packed with sheets and towels.

Nowadays, as I find it difficult to hang heavy curtains on the line, our daughter takes them home in the kit bag to wash and bring back.

OLIVE ROBERTS

I took two to Madame Perdrisot at the school house, on the understanding that she cook one of them for us on Christmas Day.

On the day, she arrived bearing a large silver tureen - the aroma was magnificent as she removed the cover. There was roast chicken, brussels sprouts and turnips. We thanked her and gave her a packet of cigarettes to be smoked after the family's Christmas dinner.

We ate our Christmas dinner by the handful, all sitting round on the floor, and not bothering with mess tins.

Afterwards we made tea in an old tin, with Carnation milk, but no sugar - which seemed strange as in England we had had the most delicious Christmas dinners, but no tea.

Later I wrote home for a tin of coffee (which arrived disguised as cigarettes) and Madame and her friends held a coffee party - their first in four years. I was the honoured guest having tea.

JOHN WOODROW

HAM - SORRY, RABBIT-BURGERS!

I WORKED in the NAAFI and when the Americans came over in the war, I was asked to help to open a canteen for them.

We were slightly horrified at what we saw as their lack of discipline, but the 'boys' were far more polite to us than our own lads were.

It was 'Yes, ma'am' and 'No, ma'am', and their generosity was overwhelming - if we had no cigarettes, someone would appear with a whole carton.

They could be quite patronising about our 'antique' equipment, but we took no notice.

They did not eat much - their main demands were for apple pie and coffee.

CHRISTMAS AT CALAIS

IT was near Christmas 1944, and we were at Calais, billeted at a former infants school, where we made the acquaintance of its former headmistress, Madame Perdrisot, and her husband.

We were tired of eating dehydrated and tinned food, and one day when we were out collecting stores, we called at a farm and swapped a pair of army boots for six chickens.

Then the canteen manageress had a bright idea - hamburgers! (Remember, they were strange to us then.)

I said that all we had was some cooked rabbit. She insisted, saying we could camouflage it with onion or tomato. It was difficult, but I managed to make the meat stick, although it was liable to break up.

As luck would have it, the first person into the canteen that day was the camp comedian. Of course, he wanted to try my hamburger. Naturally, he opened the bun to inspect the contents, which had broken up a bit.

He made a few odd remarks, but ate it all and came back, saying that it was a funny-looking hamburger but it tasted good.

I was so ashamed of making rabbit hamburgers that I hid in the pantry and cried.

MARY MAGEE

A NICE CUP OF KIE

WE don't hear much about cocoa these days, except as a nightcap.

But the words "Would you like a cup of kie, mate?" were music to my ears one dark night in 1943. 'Kie' was the sailors' slang for cocoa.

It was on a tank landing craft, a few hours before we were due to land on the Sicilian coast. We were loaded with self-propelled guns and I was the driver of one of them.

It had been a rough passage all the way from North Africa, and nearly all the gunners were seasick, some worse than others.

My condition was about 'middling'. I kept myself on the move as much as I could, but I couldn't help wondering what condition we would all be in when the time came to hit the beach.

I could hear the faint sound of voices above me, and looking up saw what looked like a 'crow's nest'. A couple of sailors were

inside enjoying a chinwag and a fag.

My face must have looked a little green because one of the sailors said: "Would you like a cup of kie, mate?"

I didn't know that 'kie' was cocoa, but as it seemed to be a warming drink, I said: "Not half".

Well, that magic potion did the trick, and I was as right as rain in no time.

There was enough for my mate as well, and to this day, I am sure that when the invasion of Southern Europe started, our two self-propelled guns were the steadiest to be driven up that Sicilian beach.

JACK ROLFE

BUSMAN'S HOLIDAY

DURING my National Service in 1950, I was stationed at Compton Basset, Wiltshire, as a teleprinter operator.

We had a pass to go home every weekend, but the official coach fare to London was 17s return, more than most of the lads could afford on a regular basis.

So I did a deal with a coach company to hire 32-seater coaches for £20. It worked out at 12s 6d per passenger, and I charged each one 13s, which allowed me a free seat as the organiser, with a little left over for a tip to the driver.

Many of the lads could not afford the 13s fare, though. So by agreement with the driver, we hit on the idea of allowing them to sit on the floor down the centre of the coach for a return fare of 8s - which went to the driver as he was taking the risk of breaking the law.

One week, we got wind that the police had been tipped off about this practice, so we put the extra passengers in the boot of the coach for the first part of the journey.

You can imagine their faces when they were let out. They must have been half-suffocated.

DEREK BOSWELL

BALLOON GIRLS

Win Cosens (nee Ford) has happy memories of being stationed at the wartime balloon site 115 at Whitworth Park, Manchester.

She is pictured here second right on the back row and her friend Margaret Jennings is second on the left.

The picture is not as idyllic as it seems - the group was soon to be broken up.

"We were due to be made obsolete and had to retrain as flight mechanics, cooks or drivers," she writes.

"Margaret became a driver and I trained as a flight mechanic.

"I met my late husband on the balloon site. He was a soldier on a training course at REME in Manchester."

NARROW ESCAPES

CLOSE TO DISASTER

I WAS one of the command post detachment of the Home Guard in the Manchester area which used radar belonging to the regular battery some distance away from our own anti-aircraft rocket projector site. We had our own plotting table, and late one evening we received a message from HQ that a Bullseye exercise had begun.

This gave the Home Guard and the regular anti-aircraft battery a chance to practise with live targets, and involved a training run for Bomber Command planes to seek out large towns and practise bombing.

We were immediately put on the alert for the exercise, so we manned our instruments and awaited instructions.

Our officer called the other command post and asked for the officer in charge. He was told that he was not there. Our officer told the telephonist to call out the gunners to action stations, and to man the projectors and issue the orders which were to follow. Meanwhile, someone was dispatched to the nearest pub to find the missing officer and tell him what was happening.

We identified the planes' movements on our plotting table and gave our readings to the officer, who relayed them as instructions to the other command post.

We came to the order 'Stand by'. The next one would be 'Fire'. Suddenly the missing officer rang us up, asking what it was all about.

"Bullseye target practice," he was told.

"Good God, man, they've loaded live

rounds!" he shouted - and immediately cancelled all the instructions.

There were 64 projectors on the site, each one carrying two rockets. If the order to fire had been given, at least 64 rockets would have caused havoc to the practising planes. Little did they know how close they had come to disaster!

V CUMMINGS

A SCARE AT THE ENSA PARTY

ON December 23,1943 my mates and I went to a party held by members of ENSA on the troop ship Leopoldville, in the Atlantic. We were bound for West Africa.

They were giving a show in the canteen, when suddenly the whole ship shook. We could hear the vessel's metal plates banging. The girls on the stage screamed and went pale.

Then we heard the alarm calling us to muster to boat stations: Submarine warning.

All the previous boat station practices we'd had seemed to be completely forgotten. I thought there was going to be a panic - many people rushed towards the stairs in order to get on deck, blocking the only way out. The women were screaming and shouting. Just one cool-headed person shouted: "Keep calm, keep calm!"

We got our senses together and calmly made our way to our boat stations. Everybody was shaken up. Depth charges had been dropped and a submarine was in the area.

Again the ship's plates shuddered and left a ringing in our ears. I think at that moment my life passed before me as I stood on deck.

The ship was carrying many Queen Alexandra nurses.

I looked at the rafts - and realised that if the ship was hit they were not going to be enough to take us all. Some of us might survive, but most of us would perish, either from the sharks or the cold sea water.

After about an hour-and-a-half of waiting at boat stations, we heard the 'all clear'.

J THOMSON

A DANGEROUS OCCUPATION

IN 1940 I volunteered for munitions work and trained as a 'filler' for six-grain detonators and boosters for 22mm shells.

It was one of the most dangerous roles, working with explosives like fulminate and lead oxide, which turned the skin yellow. Had I dropped any of the boxes of fulminate, we would all have gone to kingdom come! Quite a few girls were blown up - mostly in the drying rooms, when things got overheated. We were given badges with 'Frontline Duty' and two crossed bombs on them.

We have never been represented in any of the parades. We played a very important part in the war and have just been ignored.

DOROTHY STOCKBRIDGE

BOMB HAPPY

IN 1944, the Japanese knew they were losing at Imphal, and put in suicidal attacks, hoping to rescue victory from defeat.

My regiment had been in the field some time. All of us were tired and overdue for a rest. My platoon was ordered on a patrol we knew would be dangerous - in my exhausted state I just accepted it without feeling.

Most patrols at this time were being shot up, so it was not long before we too came under fire from ridges to our left and in front.

The four men in front of me fell instantly. The enemy then concentrated on the men behind, who were now withdrawing.

I could hear the enemy machine guns firing furiously. I looked at the men in front - they were beyond my help.

By now I was the only one in view. I walked up a bank on my right. Bullets were hitting the ground around me. Had the enemy aimed with one shot, they would have hit me but they were spraying over open sights.

I dropped behind the bank and crawled along a few yards. Looking back, they were still churning away at the bank where they last saw me. I lay there for a few moments and started chuckling. I was 'bomb happy'.

In the horror and terror of battle, it was a pleasant feeling of euphoria.

J F CLIFFORD

A PSYCHIC COMMAND

I WAS a teleprinter operator in the WAAF. I had just finished duty one day and was walking along the camp when I suddenly heard an inner voice telling me: 'Go home'. I said: "I can't go home - I haven't a pass or leave".

However, the feeling was so strong that I just 'took off' and went home. I don't remember how - I must have caught a train.

When I arrived, my mother looked at me in amazement and said: "How have you come so quickly, love?"

My brother Harold was still in the phone box trying to contact me to ask me to come home to see him as he was on embarkation leave prior to going to Gibraltar. He was as surprised to see me as Mum - we just caught him as he came out of the kiosk.

It was the last time I saw him - he was killed in a Sunderland flying boat which crash-landed on Gibraltar shortly afterwards.

How glad I was that I obeyed that 'command' to go home when I did.

VIOLET TAYLOR

STEPPING OUT

In the centre of this trio from 43 Division, Hampshire Regiment, pictured at Margate around 1941, is Clarence Howard, then nicknamed Kelly.

A SMART MOVE

I WAS on the Hunt Class destroyer HMS Garth, which was the first large ship to sail up the Schelde after the taking of Antwerp.

We tied up at the fish dock in the centre of the city, and as port bridge lookout, I watched my messmates complete the job.

Then the skipper told the first lieutenant to move the ship a bit further down - he didn't like where we were.

I heard the men on the fo'c'sle curse, but we moved three places down and had just tied up again when a V2 rocket landed on the spot where we had been.

I often wonder how many of those on that ship - five of us were from Manchester Grammar School - are still alive and remember the incident.

DENNIS BUTTERWORTH

THE DAY WE WENT HOME EARLY

I WAS a Land Girl in the Cambridgeshire Fens, and at Easter, 1945, when we were hoeing in the fields, we asked the foreman for permission to leave work a little earlier than usual so that we could catch our trains home for the holiday weekend.

The Foreman, Mr Gilbert, teased us, saying that it depended on how well we worked during the day. We must have worked well because later in the afternoon he came along and said we could go, and wished us all a Happy Easter.

When we went back to the farm after the holiday, we were shocked to be told that there had been an air crash. A Stirling bomber had crashed in the field where we had been working - it was a good thing we had gone home earlier than we should have done.

BETTY SPRIDGEON

MY LUCKY DAY

DURING the war I was making my way back from leave, accompanied by my wife. There was a lot of crowding and confusion when we arrived at the station in the black-out, and we both landed up down in the 'well' of the lines.

A train was backing into the buffers so we had to look sharp, but helped by some kind people, we managed to get out just in time.

My CO saw that I was shaken up by the incident and gave me 10 days extra leave.

Fate was kind to me - during that time my chums were drafted without me and I heard later that they hadn't fared so well. I was drafted out to Monty and the Desert Rats.

Strange how a near-disaster at the station turned out to be my luckiest day.

JIM COLE

'TO WHOM IT MAY CONCERN'

I WAS a very young section commander serving in the Black Watch in Palestine just after VE Day. We were on patrol and under fairly accurate fire from terrorists, when I spotted one of my section running for cover in a very crouched stance, which slowed down his speed.

Later, when we had time to reflect on things, I gently admonished the soldier on his poor field training. I told him he had been watching too many American movies and said that crouching wouldn't help him because if a bullet had his name on it, it would find him!

He said it wasn't so much that bullet but the one that was marked 'To Whom It May Concern' that worried him!

This classic reply caused us many a laugh in later years, and we all carried a spent cartridge with 'To Whom It May Concern' engraved on it. Not being able to produce it when asked cost drinks all round. I still have mine after all these years.

RAY IRONMONGER

A TRIO OF ESCAPES

MY parents sent three sons off to war to serve in the Navy, the Royal Air Force and the Army.

My elder brother Arthur tramped miles to board a destroyer on the beaches at Dunkirk. Only months later he was shipped out to Egypt to join General Montgomery's final drive from El Alamein in the Western Desert.

I was already out there with the Long Range Desert Air Force, after having been trapped and abandoned in the dock area of Alexandria by Field Marshal Rommel's sudden surge. The infamous and inexplicable lull there was our salvation.

Arthur and I were able to share leaves together in Alexandria and Cairo.

My younger brother Victor boarded a destroyer which was torpedoed and sunk in the Indian Ocean, and spent six days in an open boat with three other survivors.

The worst injury he suffered was a torn cartilage received in an inter-service football match in Delhi.

BILL STOVELL

ALMOST A COLLISION

AS an 18-year-old ordinary seaman in the Royal Navy, I was serving aboard a small armed vessel in the Lewis Isles, northwest of Scotland, in February 1944, bound for the Firth of Forth.

Late one afternoon, we received a signal from Coastal Command, Scapa Flow, that the battleship King George V, accompanied by three destroyers, had just left, and would pass us at about midnight. It was a pitch black night and extremely cold.

I was look-out on the top bridge, and about midnight I spotted a movement to port. Grabbing the binoculars, I just about made out two of the destroyers.

I reported the sightings to the officer, a young sub-lieutenant no older than myself, who reckoned that the battleship must be on the far side and the other destroyer on the other side of them.

We sailed on for another few minutes when I saw what looked like a large seagull flying just on the waterline dead ahead. It grew larger as I stared.

Then I saw a huge black cliff. I screamed at the officer: "It's the King George, sir, and it's almost on top of us!" "Oh, my God," he cried. "Hard to port, hard to starboard, no, hard to port…"

Then Bob, the Asdic operator, a much older man, opened the sliding door to the bridge and pulled me outside. I went a lit-

tle way down the steel ladder fixed amidships, leaning outward ready to jump.

Fortunately for us all, the Leading Seaman was at the wheel. Using his own discretion, he swung hard to starboard, and we missed the King George's bow by no more than a few feet.

The wash rolled our small ship at least 75 per cent over. It was lucky that I was gripping the ladder tightly because my feet slid off under me. I swung out and back hard as the ship straightened up again, thankfully regaining my foothold.

The ship rolled violently for some time before settling back on an even keel.

E A HURRELL

AN ATTACK
FROM THE AIR

ABOUT a week after we arrived in the French town of Rennes in June 1940, we were given the order to evacuate and make for the coast.

We were waiting to leave from the Rennes railway junction, when we were attacked by Stuka dive bombers, and blown out of our wagons. I landed on my face by the railway line, badly gashing myself and smashing my teeth. Our CO, himself badly hurt, issued the order: "Every man for himself!"

To get away to the main road we had to cross a field and a small canal. A frightening sight met our eyes - the bodies of our lads, together with those of children, nuns, and old men who had been fishing in the canal. It was my first experience of violent and sudden death.

One of our lads, a Geordie miner and a hero in every way, had managed to find a flat-bottomed punt and was ferrying survivors across the canal to the road.

Once on the road, several of us recovered a car lying in the ditch, and set off for the coast. We were aiming to get to St Malo, but a military policeman at a roadblock told us St Malo had been taken by the Germans. He advised us to make for Brest.

We stopped at various petrol stations to try to fill up, but were always given the same answer - 'No mange, no essence'. As a last resort, our CQMS produced a revolver in order to secure supplies. It was much later that he told us he hadn't any ammunition.

We eventually reached Brest, where we managed to scramble aboard a ship just about to leave port. There were troops everywhere, even clinging to the rigging, but we made it back to Falmouth - despite being bombed as we crossed the Channel.

WILLIAM D MOORE

William Moore photographed in Rennes. The French photographer and his wife were arrested as spies a week after it was taken.